FURTHER TRAVELLERS' TALES
FROM HEAVEN AND HELL

Edited by Gordon Medcalf

Published by Eye Books

Further Travellers' Tales From Heaven And Hell
1st Edition
June 2004

Published by Eye Books Ltd
51a Boscombe Rd
London
W12 9HT
Tel/fax: +44 (0) 20 8743 3276
website: www.eye-books.com

Set in Frutiger and Garamond
ISBN: 1903070112

British Library Cataloguing in Publication Data
A catalogue record for this book is available from the British Library

Printed and bound in Great Britain by Biddles Ltd

Illustrations by Micky Hiscocks

To Robert Louis Stevenson, whose *Treasure Island* first conjured up for many of us when we were very young, all the magic, excitement, and also the perils and rewards of travelling to exotic, unknown places.

'I travel not to go anywhere, but to go.
I travel for travel's sake.'

Travels with a Donkey

Editor's Foreword

Further Travellers' Tales from Heaven and Hell, the third volume in this very popular series, is I suggest an even better read than its successful predecessors. Why should this be? The format is not dissimilar, the countries visited and the adventures described are no more wide-ranging. I believe there are two objective reasons for the extra can't-put-downability.

First, due to its past success *Heaven and Hell* has become a global event. The first competition to find the best Travellers' Tales was nationwide; the third was worldwide. This has resulted in a higher proportion than before of entries from English-speaking overseas nationals. Which enriches the mix, and also perhaps the bold, lively use of our stodgy old language.

Secondly, there has been a change to the rules of the competition whose winning entries adorn these pages. In previous editions the maximum word count was 500 words. This time the limit has doubled, an opportunity of which many of our winners took full advantage.

This extra length works well, provided (if you will pardon the old saucy innuendo) you know how to use it. It does permit just a smidgen more development of story or character, variation of pace, or even a chance to put a little twist in the tail. Which in turn may account for the higher incidence of published authors amongst our entrants this time, whose skilfully crafted contributions contrast with the natural as-I-tell-it-down-the-pub freshness of the more anecdotal narratives. The blend of the two, again, yields a wider variety and a richer mix.

As editor I write all the fore-going with considerable authority, since no one no matter how enthusiastic and avid will ever read this book either as often or as carefully as I did during its gestation period. But no one should therefore assume my big thumbs up is inspired by my personal involvement or by pride. Relief, perhaps, but no pride.

Only the authors can and should be proud. The editor's role is simply that of the gardener's assistant: required to water, weed, trim a bit here and do a little re-potting there, but at his peril does he interfere with the basic scheme or design. Very much a supporting role, but if they dish me up so many tales by turns as heart-warming, riotous, hair-raising and mind-opening as the ones in this book - then actually pay me for reading them, who am I to complain?

Gordon Medcalf

GORDON MEDCALF became a freelance writer and editor in 1990, after two successful business careers: first in marketing (at Procter & Gamble, Gillette and G-Plan Furniture, where he was marketing director), and secondly in the advertising business (where he was team leader on many famous campaigns, including Beanz Meanz Heinz, Be a Cadbury's Fruit & Nut Case and Join the Professionals).

He writes mainly for businesses and business publications, and his editing work has been mostly in the fields of travel and marketing. For Eye Books his credits include successes like Riding the Outlaw Trail, Desert Governess and Frigid Women.

Contents

1	WITHOUT PERMISSION	1
2	BORED? IN FLORIDA?	5
3	THE MUFFIN WAR	9
4	FIREBALL	13
5	PARADISE LOST	17
6	THE DAY I STOOD IN LENIN'S BATH	21
7	VISIBLE FROM THE MOON?	25
8	WHERE IS WILLIAM?	29
9	LUNATIC IN LIMA	33
10	TEMPUS FUGIT	37
11	THE SEVEN MILE HITCH	41
12	BIG TIGER	43
13	WRONG PLANE!	47
14	BY TRAIN ACROSS RAJASTHAN	51
15	PUMPKIN SOUP	53
16	BORDER LUNACY	57
17	DOORWAY TO DISEASE	59
18	LAST TAKE-OFF FROM BAGHDAD	63
19	A NEAR RUN THING	67
20	BOREDOM: THE GREAT ESCAPE	71
21	ROAD RAGE IN ISTANBUL	75
22	BAGGAGE PARTY	77
23	SIKH AND YOU SHALL FIND	81
24	LOVE AND WATER	85
25	NURSE	89
26	LE FAWLTY TOWERS FRANÇAIS?	91
27	UPSIDE DOWN OVER QUEENSTOWN	93
28	FUNNY MONEY	97
29	THE SKY BURIAL	101
30	CINEMA PAKISTANO	105
31	HOLY SHIT!	109
32	VINCENT LOUIS	111
33	A MUSICAL MONK	115

34	TICKED OFF	117
35	A FRIENDLY GAME IN KL	121
36	THE ESCAPE COMMITTEE	125
37	AN ARCTIC SWIMMING LESSON	127
38	A TRAVELLING POM	131
39	AUDIENCE WITH A SEER	135
40	BIRDING HEAVEN	139
41	BIRDING HELL?	141
42	WELCOME TO AMERICA	145
43	DROWN AND OUT	149
44	OASIS OF PEACE	153
45	A CLOSE SHAVE IN SEVILLE	157
46	BUS RIDE IN TANZANIA	159
47	A BEIJING PICKLE	161
48	THE JOYS OF CANOE CAMPING	165
49	THE EARTHENWARE PHIAL	169
50	ROCKET FUEL	171
51	THE RIVER GOD	173
52	ANYONE FOR SHUFFLEBOARD?	177
53	IMAGES OF CAIRO	179
54	CHINESE WATER TORTURE	183
55	THE CURSE OF APACHE	185
56	PICTURES COME TO LIFE	189
57	A PAINFUL OUTING	193
58	VIETNAM: A LONG WAY TO GO	197
59	ON TOP OF THE WORLD	201
60	DOG BITES MAN	203
61	FOLLOW THAT NUN!	207
62	TITANIC OR TENEMENT?	211
63	DOC ON WHEELS	215
64	LIFE'S A BYTCH	219
65	THE EAGLE'S LAIR	223
66	ST DENNIS THE BLESSED	227
67	BORDER HOLD-UP	229
68	LEAVING TIBET	233
69	THE BANK ROBBERS	237
70	HALFWAY TO HEAVEN	241

1 WITHOUT PERMISSION

François is the husband of the French Consul. When he hears we have been filming in Nigeria without official permission, he becomes stern:

'This is a police state. Where are your tapes?'

'In my hotel.'

'You don't really expect to walk out of Kano airport with those tapes in your luggage, do you?' asks François,

'They'll be waiting for you.'

I sense the first sour stirrings of panic in my stomach.

'What do you suggest I do?' I ask, my voice small with anxiety.

François shrugs.

'Whatever you do, do not think of trying to take those tapes on the plane with you.'

Next morning I confide my fears to my local producer Ihria. He says he has no idea what to do.

'If this was Lagos, it would be easy,' he says. 'Here, I simply don't know anyone. We'll have to talk to Marliyah.'

Marliyah, who is our interpreter, has a cousin, Hassan, who works for KLM, the airline which is flying me.

We find him in the KLM office. Marliyah does not tell him we have made the film illegally because she thinks it will compromise him.

'If those tapes go through the scanner, they'll be ruined,' she says.

'Don't worry,' says Hassan, 'I'll make sure you don't have to put them through. I'll speak to the security guys myself.'

This is not working.

'Maybe instead you can take the tapes onto the plane for her?' ventures Marliyah.

Hassan narrows his eyes and looks at me suspiciously.

'What's on the tapes?' he demands.

'A film about Kano,' I say. He looks at me closely.

'Why do you want me to carry these tapes?' he asks.

'Because even if they go near the machine they will be damaged,' I repeat.

'That is not so. Many tapes and films go through our machines.'

'I think we can assure you it will be very worth your while,' Marliyah says quietly.

Hassan eyes me as if estimating my worth, while he talks to Marliyah in their own language. I feel helpless just standing there but Hassan is my only hope. Suddenly both of them break out in smiles.

'OK,' he says, turning to me, 'Come back at six o'clock with the tapes in a bag.'

God knows what Marliyah has promised him, but I know I will have to leave her with a hefty wedge of petty cash. The next step is to find a big but unobtrusive bag for the tapes. Then I remember the Prada tote bag my sister-in-law gave me for Christmas. It is big enough, and will not look out of place slung over a man's shoulder. I hand it over at six, wondering what my London employers would say if they knew I was entrusting their precious material to a virtual stranger.

Departure time arrives. Beyond the passenger barrier armed soldiers are rifling through everyone's luggage. My bag is searched twice. The first soldier uses his gun barrel to sift through my clothes. I cannot take my eyes off it. Then he ushers me towards another soldier, who asks:

'Where are the tapes?'

'What tapes?' I ask brightly, smiling and swallowing hard.

'Have you not made a film here?'

My stomach churns, but I dare not hesitate.

'No,' I say. My jaw aches from smiling.

'Show me your passport,' he demands.

He examines it, looking hard at the picture and then at me and back again. He orders a third soldier over, who searches my bag again.

'You have no tapes?' asks soldier number three. This one smiles disarmingly.

I think my legs may give way. I feel light-headed.

'OK,' he says suddenly. 'Go.'

He shoves my clothes back into my bag and zips it up. But it isn't over.

Hassan has told me he will meet me in the departure lounge but I cannot see him. I wonder if I can even remember what he looks like. My flight is called. I have a last desperate look round, but there is nothing for it but to go to the departure gate. A jolly, plump KLM official is tearing our boarding passes.

'Hassan will meet you by the plane,' he says under his breath. He does not once look up. I think I may have imagined it. I look round to see if anyone else has heard, but the other passengers are making their way out. We start across the tarmac towards the plane, and I see several soldiers with guns standing round the foot of the plane steps. I feel sick.

Through the crowd of passengers I spot Hassan. As we inch closer I see he does not have my bag. He stands next to a soldier. I draw level with him. As soon as he sees me he grins. He walks nonchalantly over to a KLM car, opens the boot and takes out my Prada bag. He brings it over to me, right under the eyes of the soldiers.

'Have a good flight,' he says.

I make it up the steps in a trance. I could kiss the smiling air stewardess who points the way to my seat. I stow the precious bag with its illicit contents in the overhead locker. I sit down, sweating and wait. The doors close, and for the first time I start to feel safe. Then the Captain announces a short delay. The doors re-open and four armed soldiers come down the aisle, peering closely at everyone as they move steadily towards me. I feel sick. I shut my eyes and hear my heart pounding. Minutes later they leave the plane. I see them on the tarmac, lighting cigarettes and laughing, their guns slung casually over their shoulders. The doors re-close, the engines roar and the plane takes off. I promise myself that never again will I film without permission in a police state. It is a promise I have kept.

Charlotte Metcalf, Film-maker, England

Favourite Hobbies: Travel, film, reading, writing

Favourite Country: Don't have one - too many

Favourite Book: Hundreds

Other Publishing Experience: One Book - Walking Away

2 BORED? IN FLORIDA?

It sounded like the chance of a lifetime: Port St. Lucie, Florida, for a month, for nothing.

Some friends of friends of friends who lived out there were coming over to England for a month, and wanted someone to housesit their very stylish four-bedroom home with air-con, swimming-pool, and use of two cars (in America, one is never enough, not even for one person). Both cars were 5-litre, V8, and did around seven gallons to the mile.

My end of the deal was that I pay for my flight over and once there, look after their cat Tuna. That aside I could work away on my next novel in peace and quiet. In sunny Florida, home of Disneyworld, alligators, Miami Vice and Tropicana orange juice.

The house was nice enough, the pool small but warm and inviting, and Tuna was a good companion. It all seemed OK. So after a first morning's work, I decided to go for a walk around the neighbourhood.

Big mistake. I walked down the street and turned into another street. It was nice, but it looked much like the first street. I walked on a while longer, and then into another street. It looked much like the second street. And the first street. In fact every street for the next thousand miles? was identical. Lined with nice single-storey houses, surrounded by well-watered gardens, pools out the back. And not a soul around, let alone anyone out walking.

I walked on. There were no shops, no bars, no restaurants. Just more houses. It was June, in Florida, and humidity was 70%. I was getting hot, but I walked on with grim determination, determined to find something. But there was nothing. I began to feel a little bored.

Port St. Lucie, like most American towns, has no centre. Instead it has strips. The nearest strip to my house that was really any good was eight miles. I tried cycling it but I nearly got killed. London is a paradise for cyclists compared to Florida. So I had to drive.

There was only one place in town worth going, they said. The Port St. Lucie Blues Bar you gotta go there! So I went. Contents: a smoking hippy playing an electric organ. Three middle-aged couples eating their pointlessly huge meals that they'd never be able to finish. And a guy at the bar. I went to sit at the bar.

He heard me order a pint of Guinness.

'You Australian?'

'Er, no English.'

'So where in England you from?'

'I'm from London.'

'London, OK.' He nodded.

'Well, I live in London. I'm from Cheltenham originally. Over towards Wales.'

'Wales. Hunh. In the west of England, right?'

'Well, Wales is the country that's west of England. That bit that...'

'I thought Wales was a siddy.'

'Er, no ... no, a country.'

'Hunh.'

Strangely offended, the guy sank down towards his beer and didn't speak to me again.

Ninety-five per cent of Americans never go abroad. Those that do - the ones you see in St Mark's Square, Venice, Idderley, with their loud shirts, Bermuda shorts and arses the size of Kansas - they are the *crème de la crème*. They are America's cultural élite.

I didn't think Port St. Lucie had a cultural élite.

By Day Three I was dying of boredom.

Sixteen miles from Port St. Lucie was a beach called Hobe Sound. Mile upon mile of pure white sand under a blue, blue sky. The sea was ridiculously warm. Coconuts brought by the Caribbean currents washed up along the shore. And you could lie there and watch ospreys diving for fish as many as a dozen at a time. You don't get to see ospreys in the UK, unless you're very, very lucky, and in Scotland. Here they were as common as herring gulls. Here you could watch the ospreys actually having aerial dogfights with the pelicans. And sometimes, out to sea, you'd glimpse a shiny black dorsal fin slicing through the water and you'd wonder: shark or dolphin?

But, and this was the funny thing, there was nobody else here. Not a human soul. It was just me and the pelicans and the ospreys. Yet we were only half an hour's drive from Port St. Lucie one way, and Stuart the other - a hundred thousand people lived nearby. But not one came here. So, although Hobe Sound was staggeringly beautiful and wild, it was also kind of lonely. Why was nobody here?

I knew the answer. They weren't here because Hobe Sound was a nature reserve. And that meant that to get here you had to park the car some way back, and walk. Walk for as much as twenty minutes to get to the immaculately protected, ecosensitive beach. And twenty minutes walking was too much. Instead, the one hundred thousand inhabitants of Port St. Lucie and Stuart were all down at their grotesquely distended shopping malls, wearing training shoes with little red flashing lights in the soles, contemplating buying a fourth television, and burping up the taste of their 'Tex-Mex Monster Chicken'n'Cheese two-pounder Tortilla Wrap, dusted with Cajun-Style Spices, and Covered with a Succulent Melted Topping of Cheddar-Style Cheese.'

None of them - not one - wanted to walk along the beach at Hobe Sound and watch the ospreys.

Not so very long ago, I thought, their Pilgrim Fathers, Oregon Trail-blazers and Pike's Peak or Busters were tough, determined, self-denying, hardworking, thrifty, brave, and fantastically adventurous. But only a few generations on their descendants have slumped back in their Laz-E-Boy™ reclining chairs, flicked on the cable TV shopping channels, and now sit there guzzling their way through their Jumbo-Size Ben 'n' Jerry's deep-fried chocolate-chip pizza with Xtra Pepperoni.

And that is their idea of what the American Dream was all about. That was why their forefathers made their arduous trek from sea to shining sea.

O my America my Newfoundland!

Christopher Hart, 38 years old, Novelist and journalist, England

Favourite Hobbies: Hiking, travel, painting

Favourite Country: Ireland

Favourite Book: Moby Dick by Herman Melville

Other Publishing Experience: Various travel articles for newspapers. Three novels - The Harvest, Rescue Me and Julia

3 THE MUFFIN WAR

When an American hiker turned up missing in Taiwan, where I live, I found myself leading what turned out to be a four day search party. Over this period I climbed more than twenty kilometres a day up and down the mountains. It was not the mileage, nor the mountains, nor the altitude that finally defeated me, it was ordering breakfast in Tien Shan.

A curious anomaly in Taiwan is the collective English vocabulary. The concept that a word could have more than one meaning hasn't reached the linguistically challenged islanders yet. When they use a dictionary, if they use one at all, they always take just the first and most literal meaning of any word, ignoring all the other notes and options. So, for example, if they see a warning sign which says: 'Use discretion when entering the construction site', they take this to mean that they have to enter secretly, or at the very least, that they musn't tell anyone they have been there.

It is possible there is only one English dictionary in Taiwan, because amazingly they are very consistent, and all use the precisely the same faulty translations. For example, all Taiwanese translate the word for 'alcohol', as 'wine'. When they offer you a drink in English they say something like:

'Which kind of wine would you like: beer, whisky, or Burgundy?'

The latest faulty mistranslation to hit Taiwan, has been the word 'muffin.' Suddenly, there are muffins on every menu, in both Taiwan and China. But when it reaches the table it is a waffle. Who told them a waffle was called a muffin? I don't know. And how this mistake has been so widely perpetuated is also a mystery. But there it is, further proof that they are a robotic people, capable only of imitation.

When I sat down to breakfast at the Catholic Youth Centre in Tien Shan I was in the mood for waffles, so naturally I ordered a muffin.

Now the Taiwanese don't know what to put on waffles aka

muffins. They serve them with a variety of toppings ranging from fresh fruit, to tuna, to pork floss. The latter is made of shredded pork, flavoured with some nameless substance which infallibly triggers the gag-reflex in all foreigners. I don't know what they do to wholesome pork to make it so unpalatable, but I would sooner let people beat me with sticks than eat a single helping of pork floss. Unbelievably, this masochistic concoction, straight from Satan's kitchen, is a favourite Taiwanese muffin topping.

Ironically, the one substance you will never see on a muffin/waffle is maple syrup. You also won't get butter, but you might get jam, which is of course called jelly, American-style.

As I adapted slowly to the culture I have acquired a taste for waffles with peanut butter. It may sound strange, but it is the only chance I ever get to eat peanut butter here, and as a topping it beats the hell out of pork floss, deep-fried chicken butt or other unmentionables.

When I ordered my muffin the reaction I got from the waitress convinced me, once again, that Taiwan will very soon find itself a province of mainland China.

'We can't put peanut butter on a muffin,' said the waitress.

'I just saw you serve peanut butter to that other table.'

'Yes, but they ordered toast. We can put peanut butter on toast.'

'So, put peanut butter on a muffin!'

'I can't.'

'Why? Because you don't know how? The little holes trip you up? It's really the same concept. Just put some on the knife, slap it on, and smear.'

'No! I can't put peanut butter on yours because it is a muffin.'

'I see.'

I paused. What could I say? The peanut butter was inches away from her left hand, and the muffin was inches away from her right hand. And yet she was unable to put them together. Should these people really be allowed to govern themselves? In China if the price was right they would have slaughtered their own grandmother, whipped her to a foamy froth, and smeared her on a muffin or anywhere else for that matter.

I worked out a plan:

'Fine,' I said, and ordered a toast with peanut butter, and a muffin with jelly (a waffle with jam).

She dutifully wrote down the order and returned to the kitchen. For her it was settled but for me, well I just couldn't let it go. I stuck my head into the kitchen:

'Instead of putting jelly on the muffin and peanut butter on the toast, could you just do it the other way round, please?'

'No.'

Have they been brain-washed by the Secret Muffin Police? Clearly rules are rules and must be obeyed.

When my order came I was just about to execute my cunning Plan B, which was to do it myself: to smear the peanut toast onto the waffle. A masterstroke. They didn't know who they were up against.

But just then, two cops walked in. Oh, they looked casual enough, like they were just stopping by for breakfast. But I knew why they were there. The girl had pressed the concealed button behind the counter. The Muffin Police were just waiting, taunting me - daring me to try and eat my waffle with peanut butter. If I did, my feet would not touch the ground, and there would have been one less annoying foreigner poking his nose into a case that everyone else wanted to see closed. They'd have packed me off in a second, with orders never to return to Tien Shan, 'or else!'

In the fat, easy life of the resident Americans a muffin was just a waffle. But here, in this miniature police state called Tien Shan, it was a political statement.

Slowly, reluctantly, I ate my waffle with jam. And with it, for extra flavour, I had to eat my pride. They had won.

Antonio Graceffo, Taiwan, 36 years old, Adventure writer

Favourite Hobbies: Writing, adventure sports, studying languages, martial arts

Favourite Country: Thailand

Favourite Book: The Old Man and the Sea, The Little Prince, The Quiet American, Silk and Steel, Wind Sand and Stars

Other Publishing Experience: Various adventure articles and two books - The Monk from Brooklyn and The Desert of Death on Three Wheels

4 FIREBALL

This morning our Jensen Interceptor, our pride and joy, blew up.

I mean it turned into a fucking *fireball*, which we escaped by seconds.

Today was to have been another long journey - 230 miles up the road to Barcelona - but we hadn't gone three miles when it happened, without warning. We were doing I suppose forty miles an hour, when suddenly the car was full of smoke. I swung across onto the hard shoulder, shouting at Ali to undo her seatbelt, and screeched to a halt. Checking Ali was on her way out of the car, I leapt out of my side. As I got out, I looked back through the windscreen over the wheel and saw, through the louvres in the bonnet, an orange-red inferno in the engine bay.

I saw Ali was past the boot on her way to safety, and I then did the stupid thing they always tell you not to do - I went back. I pivoted on one foot, and reached back into the car, swept my wallet and phone off the central console, and then made a dash for it.

I suppose I'd just passed the rear bumper, moving well, when I heard a sort of 'whump!' from behind and felt a blast of heat on my shoulders. Not looking back until I'd got twenty yards away, I then saw a huge ball of flame erupting from the front of the car, and within three or four seconds the whole car forward of the front seats was engulfed.

The next few minutes remain a bit of a blur. Ali says I was leaping up and down shouting 'No! Fucking *NO!!*', and then running back up the carriageway waving my arms to stop the traffic, shouting 'Emergentheea! EmergenTHEEA!' It's funny how even one's rudimentary grasp of language fails one in a real emergentheea.

Cars and vans were stopping - well they would; by now the flames from the Jensen were thirty feet long and spewing across all three carriageways, blown by a strong sideways wind. The motorway was already jammed, and all we could do was stand and watch her burn, while we waited for the *bomberos* to arrive. Ali couldn't watch - she sat in tears on the crash barrier. I could hardly watch, but I had this awful feeling that the tank was going to blow, and lift the car off the tarmac in slow motion to perform some spectacular mid-air pirouettes.

The fire began to eat its way back towards the tank - the whole cabin was now ablaze - and I really thought it was a matter of seconds before she went up. The bonnet was producing great gouts of flame like the footage you see of the surface of the sun and I knew then that it was beyond saving.

Everything we had for three months was in that car - clothes, cameras, shoes, hats, CD player, CDs, diaries, money - dear God, our *passports!* I just *couldn't believe* this had happened, and it was much too soon for all the implications to sink in.

Eventually - actually I don't suppose it was much more than seven or eight minutes - the *bomberos* arrived in force and efficiently and methodically doused the flames. The Guardia Civil were there too, and soon had at least two carriageways open for people to continue on their way with a juicy story to tell.

It was a mess.

The front of our beautiful Jensen had melted into the tarmac. Most of the paint had burned off, and the inside was just a charred skeleton of metal and seat springs. Here the blackened remains of a Nike trainer, there a melted CD. The seats were gone, and on what had been the back seat were the dark, misshapen lumps that had been our carry-around bags. Mine was prised out by one of the firemen, and we took the sorry remains over to the hard shoulder while Ali's was disentangled from the wreckage.

As expected, the DV video camera, my Nikon 35mm, the spare tapes, batteries, films, tripod and cables had melted to buggery, but unbelievably the inside pocket, with all our documents, travellers cheques and passports had escaped the worst of it, and although singed and brittle with heat, they were still usable. Even this very diary was a trifle blackened, but had survived. All of it must have been mere seconds from destruction when the *bomberos'* foam had puffed into action.

But everything else in the main cabin of the car had gone. Hats, shoes, maps, guide books, car manuals, a box of spare parts for the Jensen, the portable CD player and 36 CDs, Ali's make-up case and (tragically) the beginning of her book about the trip all were consumed by the awesome power of the fire. Remarkably Ali's jewels and most of our clothes, in the boot, appeared salvageable, albeit badly smoke-blackened and in need of a serious clean, though the cases that protected them had more or less melted.

We had a session with the Guardia, who were extremely Civil given the mess we had made of their motorway, and with the help of the AA, who played a blinder by phone from Hemel Hempstead or wherever, everything got sorted - we just had to sign a couple of papers. The ruined remains of our noble Jensen passed into the hands of a lurking scrap-metal dealer (who must have thought it was Christmas), and the cops even whistled up a taxi to take us, soot-stained and steaming gently, back to the Monte Picayo Hotel.

I'm writing this in bed at about eleven at night. Ali is trying to sleep, but I cannot. I can still hear the crackle and roar; still smell the acrid carbon stench; still feel the anger and frustration; still shake from the nearest I've knowingly been to death.

However, we're alive, and that has to be the most important thing. We are whole, physically undamaged, together, and although very shaken, we're alright.

Jonathan Booth, 44 years old, Internet video pioneer, England

Favourite Hobbies: Movies, cards, golf, cricket

Favourite Country: England

Favourite Book: The Hobbit

Other Publishing Experience: One book - The European Job, numerous film reviews and trade articles

5 PARADISE LOST

It seemed a good idea at the time, I mean, going on a Fiji Holiday with a feisty two year old who can't sit still for more than fifteen seconds and hates being cooped up in small places - what could possibly go wrong?

Watch this space.

I should have twigged when Betty screamed like a wounded banshee throughout the plane trip, while the rest of our party tried to pretend we didn't exist. Then there was the thrill of arriving in the middle of the night with her slumped over me, burning up with a fever. When we got to our room, naturally the cot I'd ordered wasn't there. I put my sick child into my bed and poured a stiff drink. The first of many.

I woke to the sound of someone screaming like their teeth were being extracted by an apprentice dentist with Parkinsons. It was only six o'clock, and there was my darling, sitting up to her neck in runny poo. I frantically pulled her out and into the bathroom to wash her down, which only increased the volume, so we dashed outside to walk on the beach. We had to fill in time before breakfast, but of course when we got there, there wasn't enough room for us to sit with our companions. Which came to be the pattern of the holiday.

Betty's favourite holiday trick was to run pell mell down the angled aisle in the restaurant which, as you can imagine, challenged even the most seasoned professional Fijian waiters, known for their sunny smiles and persistent charm. We sought solace by the pool, but Betty's antics were not going down gangbusters with the other guests. I asked advice from the other mothers about the rapidly spreading rash that had sprung up on her body and was reassured that it was probably heat rash - but of course to a first-time mother in the throes of an anxiety extravaganza, it was an Obscure and Potentially Fatal Tropical Disease.

So, we went to the hotel playground for a bit of fun, where Betty managed to bash her chin on the metal bar of the see saw and her temporarily chirpy state was again reduced to that of a grizzling, snotty misery-guts.

Evening couldn't come quick enough for me, and I arranged to meet the others at seven. Well, by the time I had Betty asleep and the charming babysitter ensconced it was about 7.30, and when I got to the restaurant they had gone. Instead of bursting into tears I decided to have another, even stiffer drink, and I sat in the other restaurant at a table for one, feeling like Steve Martin in *The Lonely Guy*, when they shine the spotlight on his aloneness.

Next day our companions were leaving for a few days on another island. That was when the real fun started. Everyone was around the pool, about to leave to get ready for their plane. Betty was standing at the top of some concrete steps. I turned, to see her twist, slip and then fall down the concrete steps on her face. As I ran to her, she did her standard Betty thing of leaping up and then running. Running away from the pain. Screaming. Around cosy couples in their deckchairs, past waiters with full trays of drinks, she sped away from me as fast as I could chase her.

Eventually I nabbed her, picked her up sideways like a carpet and took her down to the sea. She was still sobbing hysterically and her face was swelling up like a balloon. By the time the last remaining member of our party got back with the Arnica, the waves were doing their trick and Betty was sitting, still looking like Elephant Girl but no longer sounding like her.

Well, the others all departed, and we were left to our own fun. We got through about six ice-blocks that afternoon to bring the swelling down, and she snivelled quietly as I wheeled her around in her pushchair. That night I had room service dinner, and put her to bed early. I then launched a ferocious attack on the mini-bar before collapsing myself.

Next morning dawned sunny, bright, and diabolical. I opened my eyes to the sounds of sobs, and there was my baby, this time covered in blood and snot. The grazes on her face were more apparent now the swelling had gone down, and she'd been lying on her face which had re-started the bleeding. Off we went down to the beach for our early morning escape. The sun was glaring in her eyes so I let her out of her pushchair for a romp in the sea. Well, I might as well have just thrown her down another set of stairs.

She promptly fell over in the sand, rubbed her face with her hand, grazed the cuts, and set up a squalling that could only be mistaken for some poor creature's death throes. I shoved her under my arm, carpet-like again, and dragged the pushchair through the ankle-deep dry sand back to our room. Which seemed like a scene from Lawrence of Arabia it took so long - the only thing missing was Peter O'Toole or (better still) Omar Sharif coming to my rescue.

Safely back in our room, I had to wash her face. As Betty was inconsolable, giving a convincing impression of someone having an epileptic fit, I had to pin her down on the bed, my knees on her shoulders so she couldn't move, while I washed and then applied Savlon to the mangled nose and upper lip.

There followed a few days of wheeling Betty around grimly, to sympathetic but rather suspicious looks from the other guests (should we shop her for child abuse?). Eventually her wounds healed, and she cheered up considerably. I really can't remember much of what we did in those last few days. I've never been so pleased to leave an idyllic island resort.

Callie Blood, 42 years old, Musician / writer / mother, New Zealand

Favourite Hobbies: Food, painting, wine, reading, giggling with my daughter, singing, expanding my shoe collection

Favourite Country: New Zealand

Favourite Book: A Fine Balance by Rohinton Mistry or The House of Mirth by Edith Wharton

Other Publishing Experience: Countless jingles, songs, and children's stories, as well as various articles for magazines and newspapers

6 THE DAY I STOOD IN LENIN'S BATH

Vladimir Lenin's bath looked very clean. I can testify to this because not only was my reflection clear in the eighty-year-old chrome taps, but my warm sock-clad feet were beginning to dull the gleaming porcelain tub.

Now before an outcry of 'desecration' goes up, let me explain.

We were in Russia to make a film on Stalin for the BBC, and we had been filming drama sequences in Lenin's dacha, twenty or so miles south of Moscow. Access so far had been superb. As well as a cameraman I am also a bit of a history buff. For years the whereabouts of the dacha would have been kept secret from your average Russian. Now I found myself with a British producer and a Russian crew standing in a Museum of the Revolution.

A heavily worn leather sofa, as sat on by Stalin, the aged material torn and fading. Lenin's desk, left exactly as it was in a photo of him reading a copy of *Pravda*. Behind are row after row of books in both Russian and English, on topics that range from Karl Marx to the history of the British trade union movement. Letters written by Stalin held nervously in our hands; their colour an ageing brown, their smell of decay lingering on our fingers.

Across the corridor Lenin's old wheelchair waits under a staircase. A handrail on the stairs, fitted to help the ailing man up to his bedroom, is tapered and worn at the end where a hand has grasped a thousand times. Amidst all of this is a Russian Curator with very acceptable English, who does not seem to mind where we walk, sit or look. It is a history buff's paradise.

Back to the hotel in Moscow and you move forward a thousand years, but getting there has not changed that much. Through the permafrost on our minibus windows you still see silhouettes of figures shuffling and stamping in the frozen, dreary December light, waiting patiently for an eventual bus.

But the capital itself has changed beyond recognition. Since I was last here Muscovites seem to have found a new confidence. It is not just the smart boutiques and designer label shops that have sprung up, but also restaurants everywhere. In the early eighties Moscow had no more than a dozen restaurants (and I use the word loosely), all state run and most offering dubious food. Now you can taste food from all parts of the Old Russian Empire (best not to ask for Chechen though) and all for non-exorbitant prices.

The hotels too are changing. Ours, with a spectacular breakfast view of the Kremlin, had rooms in which you could have woken up anywhere in the world. Okay, so there were a thousand rooms, and I know that some rooms are still as they were when Stalin lived across the road, but they are becoming more rare. The mean looking, hunched and terror-inducing *babushkas* (Russian women of a certain age whose prime job always seemed to be to sit at the end of every hotel corridor glowering at every guest) have gone and been replaced by small bars offering freshly cooked and piping hot borsch washed down with copious amounts of Russian beer.

But some things are forever the same. The phone still rings in your room and a voice in rather good English offers you a pretty woman just as soon as the security man by the lift can be bribed. Before I have politely declined the offer, the telephone at the other end is slammed down with a shudder that in the old days would have made the tape machines bugging your phone jump.

Dressing before going out into -25 degrees needs some planning. First, your thermals, followed by a pair of salopettes, then on top goes a good, thick rugby shirt, a pair of cord trousers, three fleeces (yes, three) and two pairs of socks. Having got this far and hopefully having remembered to use the loo first, on go the tubes - totally and utterly essential. These are thick scarf-like, circular, brightly-coloured lengths of material. One goes around your neck and the other up over the ears and on top of your head.

Next is a pair of Arctic boots which are invaluable, but cause much merriment as you walk through reception. Then a rabbit fur hat (again, ignore the laughter), two pairs of gloves and you are ready to head out. If you did not sweat whilst walking inside the excessively heated hotel, the somewhat harsh temperature drop can actually seem rather pleasant - briefly that is.

We are lucky. Back at Lenin's dacha we do not have too much to shoot outside. Fortunately for us, the old Communists knew how to heat the insides of their country retreats well. My colleagues and I visibly shrink in size as the outdoor garb comes off.

Our friendly curator smiles ironically when our actor playing Stalin, an uncanny lookalike to the man himself, lies convincingly infirm on the floor. She is more than happy too when Lenin's lookalike fades away in the old man's real bedroom. If all this was not surreal enough, the crew laugh and joke, debating how to get the best angle for a shot.

Yes, I end up having to stand in Lenin's bath in my socks. There is no way of doing this which shows respect for the history around me, or for the legendary earthshaker himself. I am very conscious that Russians used to stand for hours outside his mausoleum, waiting to glimpse the great leader's embalmed corpse. Yet here I am, a Westerner, taking a diabolical liberty. I sneak a glance at the Curator. Fortunately she is still smiling.

Jeremy Humphries, 42 years old, Film cameraman, England

Favourite Hobbies: Writing, painting, gardening

Favourite Country: Italy

Favourite Book: Birdsong by Sebastian Faulks

Other Publishing Experience: Selection of articles for magazines and newspapers, plans to write a novel

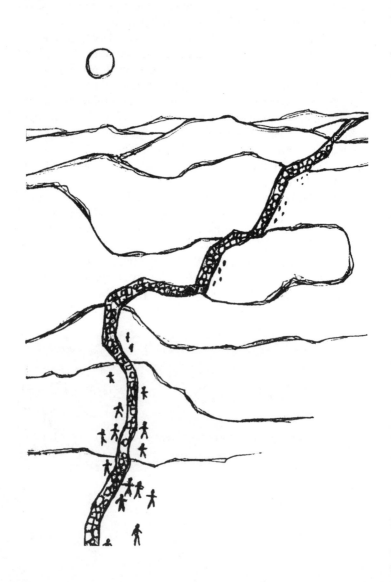

7 VISIBLE FROM THE MOON?

Most people who travel under their own steam in China will be familiar with the impossibilities of the language, bureaucracy, currency etc. That said, China is a fascinating country full of wonderful sights, if you manage to get to them. My tale is a warning to all those who shun the organised trips in favour of being 'independent'. Not for us the yellow flag-waving guides who tell you every detail of each building/tomb/rock in high-pitched, tortured English. Oh no.

Mandy and I had flown from Xi-an to Beijing. During the flight we were given a two-day-old *China Daily* to read, followed by some strange gifts, for example a can of marzipan flavoured juice which read: 'Good for lung smoothing, skin nourishing and whetting of appetite.' My appetite wasn't too whetted, which was fortunate as no proper food appeared at all.

We also received a packet of slimy brown things which turned out to be preserved plums. I never worked out exactly what they were preserved in, but they tasted horrible, even though the packet proclaimed: 'It helps digestion and refreshes oneself'. Some complimentary jasmine perfume came round, followed by strong herbal sweets 'for eliminating bad breath', which was quite timely after trying the preserved plums.

Once in Beijing we went by taxi to our hotel. Determined not to be coerced into a dreaded tour group, we strolled down to the reception desk with the nonchalance of 'seasoned travellers'.

'We'd like to arrange to visit the tourist attractions, please.'

'No ploblem. In air-condition coach with Engris-speaking guide?' asked the young lady enthusiastically.

'No thanks!' I laughed, shaking my head, 'We want to go by ourselves so we're not rushed around with a load of other people.'

'Ah. Is better you go on coach. Learn more, and velly comfortable. Good plice!'

After gentle insistence, I managed to persuade her that we really didn't want to go on a bus tour, but by private taxi, with an English-speaking driver, which worked out at the same price as the coach trip. She then produced a piece of paper and carefully wrote the following list, both in English and in Chinese characters:

Great Wall
Summer Palace
Ming Tombs

'You show to dliver.' she said. 'His name velly difficult for you to say, so we give him Western name of 'Paul'.'

The taxi arrived at nine-thirty the following morning and Mandy and I set off on our day trip.

The road out of Beijing was a brand new three-lane motorway with lengthy, complicated and artistic road signs at regular intervals, indicating that horses-and-carts/handcarts MUST stay in the inside lane, and lorries MUSN'T sound their horns (for horse-related reasons, we figured). The English M1 it was not.

Our driver's knowledge of English was virtually nil. I'd shown him the piece of paper with the destinations on and he'd beamed and nodded vigorously.

'You speak English?' I'd asked.

'Yeah-yeah!'

'Good. So, Great Wall, yes?'

'Yeah-yeah!'

And that was all he said as we drove and drove.

Eventually we arrived at an enormous, busy car park, and after some difficulty trying to tell 'Paul' how long we'd be, I drew a clock indicating we'd be two hours. He nodded and settled back for a snooze.

We ploughed excitedly into the melee of 99% Chinese day trippers to buy our tickets and then strode off to look for the

Wall. We walked round several corners and structures - no Wall. I realise that this sounds ridiculous, when the thing is so huge it is visible from the Moon, but in our ignorance, we assumed the car park and entrance were out of sight of the Wall and that soon we'd find it. Then came the question from Mandy which will be forever etched in my travel memory:

'Do you think he's brought us to the wrong Wall?'

We both collapsed with laughter. Wiping my tears, hands thrown in the air, I cried:

'How many Great Walls can there be here? We must be the only tourists who can't find the Great Wall of China! I mean, it's only 3,700 miles long, stretching to the Gobi Desert, how can we possibly miss the bloody thing?'

Eventually, in desperation, we stopped a confident-looking guide who was holding a yellow flag with an obedient gaggle of tourists behind him.

'Excuse me, do you speak English?' I asked.

'Non, Français.' he said, pleasantly. I hadn't spoken any French since high school.

'Er, *nous cherchons le grand mur.... comme ça.'* I made my hand draw big battlements in the air.

'Aah-oui! Ha, ha! Ce n'est pas ici!'

He'd understood, amazingly, and told me it was forty kilometres away by car. THIS was the Ming Tomb of the Emperor Wan-Li. He shook his head as he led his flock away, smiling sadly in disbelief.

Mandy and I felt like a real pair of supreme idiots - if we'd read our tickets we'd have seen it written in English as well as Chinese: 'Ming Tombs'. It would also have been very helpful if 'Paul' had been able to tell us that he was changing the order on our piece of paper! A look into the Ming Tombs proved rather disappointing, as most things had been removed to safety long ago during the Cultural Revolution.

The Great Wall of China, however, was overwhelmingly awesome once we got there. Its crazy zig-zag route disappearing into the distance, the angles at which parts of it were leaning, the very size of it. It was apparently started 2,000 years ago, but mostly built in the Ming Dynasty of the 14th Century. It is a huge tourist attraction, with shops, refreshments and souvenir stalls, but they didn't detract at all from the wonderful experience of climbing and walking on this amazing structure. At last, we'd made it!

Marcelle Douglas, 52 years old, School music teacher, England

Favourite Hobbies: Photography, music activities, learning to draw & sketch, travelling to new places

Favourite Country: Indonesia

Favourite Book: Running a Hotel on the Roof of the World - Five Years in Tibet by Alec Le Sueur

Other Publishing Experience: None, but keep amusing diaries of travels

8 WHERE IS WILLIAM?

I sit in my Chipmunk, F for Fox, at right angles to the beginning of the grass runway, and routinely go through the pre-flight vital actions; silently reciting as my hands move around the cockpit in synch:

'Elevator trim. Mixture. Throttle friction nut. Carb air intake. Fuel. Flaps. Hood. Harness.' And all the time part of my mind is thinking: 'Where is William?'

I press the transmitter button to speak to Ground Control - which is a single-storey shack on the edge of Kidlington Airfield:

'Fox to Tower, Take-off clearance. Over.'

'Fox, clear to go.'

I half-release the handbrake to give me differential braking, check the approach really is clear, blip the throttle to get her moving and once on the runway turn her into wind. A glance at the parking area. One Harvard, two Chipmunks, no William. He probably took off before me. No problem, we have a routine to cover this situation.

A quick mirror-check, handbrake fully off, and away we go. Throttle opened steadily all the way, holding on slight left rudder to stop her drifting to starboard as the speed builds up. I glance at the Airspeed Indicator: 35, 40, 45, and by 50 knots I have to ease the stick back, otherwise the Chippy will take off of her own accord. And that would never do. My flying instructor, an RAF Flight Lieutenant, constantly reminds me that I must fly the plane; the plane must NOT fly me.

'Not' he adds kindly, 'That she wouldn't do it much better than you.'

I obtain airfield clearance, climb away at 70 knots, and line up on the heading for Cerne Abbas, my first turning point. But where the hell is William? Only this morning, after our Anglo-Saxon tutorial, he told me he wouldn't be on the Squadron bus from Manor Road, but would ride to Kidlington on his ancient motor-bike, and see me there. Since the bus was forty-five minutes late, he must have taken off before me.

We have both opted for a triangular cross-country this afternoon, choosing very similar routes. That way we fly in company, and can mess about a bit as the whim takes us: aerobatics, formation flying, maybe beat up his Mum's home at Dorchester. Boys will be boys.

Misbehaviour, certainly. The good thing about the Oxford University Air Squadron at this time - apart from the wonder of flight and the excellent Manor Road clubhouse - is that members hold rank in the Royal Air Force Volunteer Reserve, and they actually pay you (RAF daily payscale for parade days, flying pay, annual bounty) for doing things for which, if we could, we would gladly pay THEM!

The only slight downside is that we fly the wonderful but basic Chipmunk for two years, before graduating to one of the Squadron's three precious Harvards, which are Advanced Trainers: bigger engine, much faster, retractable undercarriage, variable pitch propellor, all the gubbins. Flying by definition cannot be boring, but 120 hours in a Basic Trainer are probably too many. So we play a few unauthorised games.

But no William, no games.

Our failsafe arrangement is that if we lose touch we rendez-vous halfway between those polar landmarks Salisbury Cathedral and The Dirty Old Man of Cerne Abbas. Both quite unmissable from 5,000 feet. And when contrasted, both good for a giggle...

Now the Cathedral is behind me, the sky cloudless. William could have taken off a full half hour before me. He must be hereabouts. I circle around for a while, set up for weak cruising - 1900 r.p.m. and 85 knots, then I realise this is ridiculous. If he's already reached Cerne and turned onto the Cheddar leg, then I'm a fool. If he felt unwell and cancelled his flight, then I'm even more of a fool. I make up my mind.

My flight plan abandoned, I turn north at Salisbury and follow the roads to Marlborough, then Swindon, which I would have passed over on my final leg, so I know what heading to steer for Base. I amuse myself by singing. It's partly the sheer joy of flight, but singing into the microphone/oxygen mask attached to my flying helmet, I hear my own voice in my headphones, electronically boosted and much more flatteringly resonant than any bathroom:

'That ol' man river, he just keeps rolling alo-o-ong!'

There's a sudden crackle in my headphones, and a tense voice right in my ear:

'Baker to Tower, my engine has failed!'

My God, that's William! I'd know his voice anywhere. He sounds so close I start doing Rate Three turns, with the wings near-vertical, peering around below me for another Chipmunk. After a few minutes he transmits again, the same message with even more urgency:

'Baker to Tower, my engine has failed!'

We are all taught deadstick landings, that is gliding down without power, picking a suitable field and pretending to land, but practice is easy when you've actually got the power in reserve, and can open the throttle again any time. We none of us have any experience of a genuine forced landing, when you can't afford an error.

But William is not handling it well. His voice sounds very strained and he's completely forgotten the correct R.T. procedures - Mayday, callsign, position, and height.

Height. What can have been his altitude when he lost power? He'll have been losing height steadily since his first call. He can't stay airborne much longer. I tick off the seconds, very afraid for my friend. He could be killed. Plane crashes happen, and with less reason. If he dies I'll never fly again.

The crackle and buzz. It's William again, still in one piece:

'Baker to Tower. I say again, my engine has failed and I'm stuck at the end of the runway. Will someone please come out and get me started again, so I can take off?'

William was not early, he was very late. And that panicky urgency in his voice is not fear. It is acute embarrassment.

Edward Cecil, 70 years old, Retired marketer, England

Favourite Hobbies: Bridge; history of early Christianity

Favourite Country: France

Favourite Book: Vintage Wodehouse

Other Publishing Experience: One Book - The Brand Manager

9 LUNATIC IN LIMA

Inevitable really. When you least expect to encounter a madman, that's when one always appears. So I wasn't totally surprised in the last week of my travels when I awoke to the sound of someone chopping the legs off my bed with an axe. Across the room two other people had been tipped out of bed, and I could hear the confusion of other victims across the hallway.

'Get up you prat!'

I didn't say anything but I could see that it was Craig, a bloke I had vaguely met two nights before. He had tried to convince me to spend my last pennies in a Casino and snort two grams of cocaine.

'Come on prat, get up, you're going go-karting.'

'No, I'm not. What are you talking about?'

'It's six in the morning!' shouted a man who was trying to put his bed back together.

'You'll get yours mate. Dyson, get up you prat. It's twice you've let me down in one night. I'm going to e-mail my mate and tell him you're a poof.'

Eventually he left. I saw him six hours later looking very pale, staggering through the hallway with two litres of beer. Apparently he had crashed the go-kart.

'Don't talk to me. I feel rough,' he said.

The night before I was left in a bar at four in the morning, witnessing the antics of this madman with an equally bemused Australian.

'Fighting's my game. Got me into all sorts of scrapes.'

'Oh yeah. You box?' asked the Aussie.

'Nah, course not.'

'Wouldn't you say boxing is the best form of fighting though, mate?'

'I'll bite your snout off.'

'Ah?'

'Poke my fingers in your eyes. Stick my fingers in your ear. Come on stand up.'

He motioned for the Aussie to box him and then pushed himself against his chest.

'See? Try and box now. I've just spat your ear in your face. Got ya eye on my finger. You can't beat a pub fighter. People in boozers are the hardest in the world.'

He swiftly changed the subject to betting.

'I love a good bet me. I'll bet on anything. Anything you want. Me ol' man's the same. When we get together we can lift six men off the table in the pub. Bench press 'em. Not to mention arm wrestling. For me a good night ain't complete without a decent pint, decent arm wrestle and a bet.'

He took his shirt off and lay on the ground.

'Come on. Get on my hands. I'll lift you for a tenner.'

'No, it's all right,' I said.

'I'll do it for free, you tight prat.'

So at four-thirty in the morning I was in Lima looking into the reddening face of a lunatic as he lifted me off the ground. After this he bet the Australian that he could walk across the floor on two beer bottles.

It was a strange sight. Especially when he made the Australian face him in a press up position and began to wrestle him.

'Get at it, you prat. Me and the ol' man use to do this every Saturday in the pub. He's worse than me, best pub wrestler in England. Underground wrestling, mind. He'll wrestle all night long. Mad old prat.'

After each increasingly bizarre game he told me snippets of his life:

'Yeah, I was six months in a military prison. Don't want to talk about it. Harsh, mate. I use to train dogs. Anything from your standard guard dog to your full-blooded killers. Rip your throat out, mate. We got this big Rotweiler dosed up on drugs. I says to the gaffer: 'Let the prat at me.' You see, I had a chain on my arm. The fucker comes out meaning business and I'm saying to the gaffer 'If he jumps, club him to death.' I love dogs more than people, me.'

I managed to sneak away as he went to the toilet to snort more coke.

'Come on Dyson, just a little lightener. I've just bet that Aussie that I'll beat him at table tennis. Double or nothing. Oy, Aussie, how many hand stand press ups can you do?'

Before he left for the toilet he ran at the wall as if to go through it, just to show he didn't care.

This time it was in Lima, Peru. God knows where the next one will appear.

Matthew Dyson, 26 years old, Sales/admin for a conservation/ house restoration company, England

Favourite Country: Colombia

Favourite Hobbies: Writing, making music, playing in bands, mountain biking, comedy and travel

Favourite Book: The Post Office by Charles Bukowski

Other Publishing Experience: None

10 TEMPUS FUGIT

It was early evening and the worst of the day's heat had gone. Florence's summer crowds were drifting slowly back across the Ponte Vecchio in the direction of Brunelleschi's Duomo and the Piazza della Signoria.

The closing bell had rung and just for a few minutes I had the museum's timeless beauty to myself as I walked the linked galleries of the Pitti Palace. The thickness of the old grey walls, the depth of the Piazza Pitti and the height above street level all conspired to deaden the sounds of the slow-moving traffic below in the Via Romana.

Walking back through the delicate magic of the Palatina with no time now to stop and gaze was like glimpsing the world of Raphael, Titian and Fra Filippo Lippi through gilt-framed windows. I have asked myself a hundred times what made me turn into the pink-painted room and drew my eyes immediately to a painting of a beautiful young man. He was stunning. Thick, dark hair, sensual lips, straight nose. From his golden frame he looked down at me with all the strength, vigour and arrogance of youth. I felt weak at the knees. Wow, how I wished he could be out there for real somewhere. But the painting was from the seventeenth century so the only thing that could have lasted of this once so gorgeous man was a skeleton, maybe not even that.

The museum was closing, I had run out of time, but I continued to gaze at him. I couldn't stop. And then suddenly I seemed to hear a strange voice:

'You will get old and wrinkled, but I will always stay this beautiful.'

I turned around, there was no one, only me, and… was I going mad? I could see how the painting smiled at me. A small ironical smile. Just at the corner of the mouth, very tiny, but surely the detail of that expression had changed subtly? Probably a trick of the light.

I was not enjoying what I had seen. It was late, I must be the last visitor on this floor and I must leave at once. But somehow I couldn't, there was something holding me there. I looked again at the painting, and he was as I had first seen him, a beautiful young man with a calm face.

I took two steps back, and this time I felt a slight dizziness. Was I looking at a different painting? The man looked at least fifteen years older. About forty-five, less hair, heavier eyes, thinner cheeks. I was disoriented. It must be another portrait. But how could it be?

I wanted to leave, but instead I took another step back...

This time there was no mistake. He was now at least sixty. Full of wrinkles, and the little hair that had lasted was grey and straggly.

Trembling I stepped back yet again and confronted the face of a man to whom who life has not been kind. He looked desperately thin, tired and somehow disappointed. The eyes were empty, the mouth - formerly so sensuous - was now just a thin line, surrounded by deep-etched wrinkles.

One more step... and all I could see was a skull, a skull in a white shirt.

When my tense, retreating back touched the window behind me I started to move forward again, feeling as one does in a dream: frightened, but somehow no longer surprised. With each step I took, the old man shed years, swiftly becoming again the beautiful young stallion. Was this all a waking dream?

I don't know how long I stood in front of that portrait by Carlo Dolci (1616-86), until a badged museum attendant approached me, concerned, and asked if I was all right.

'Yes. It's a very special painting that one.' I answered, speaking with difficulty, and not reporting a word of what I felt sure I had seen and heard.

He looked at me hard, then leaned forward confidentially and murmured:

'That man you have been looking at, Signorina - he's the one we call the phantom of Palazzo Pitti.'

Titti Augustsson, 32 years old, Looking after my one year old son and in the evening I write filmscripts, Sweden

Favourite Hobbies: Horsebackriding, reading and making clothes

Favourite Country: There are so many countries that I love, I can't choose one I'm afraid

Favourite Book: My friend Muriel by Jane Duncan

Other Publishing Experience: Short stories for magazines and then there is my filmscript

11 THE SEVEN MILE HITCH

The first and the third lifts were nothing special. I was very grateful to the lady who owned the campsite just out of town and who set me on my way; a fillip for my confidence and a few miles covered. I was equally grateful to the family intent on an evening stroll at the pass and who chauffeured me through the last dozen or so hairpins. Although by then the temperature had dropped, and I was beginning to appreciate the pine and thyme scented verges and the curtain of butterflies.

The *pièce de resistance*, however, came in between.

'Where are you going?' I enquired excitedly, forgetting the basics of hitching etiquette as the slowly expiring diesel pulled up along side me.

'Where are *you* going?' two voices countered in unison. I felt they had a point.

'I'm going to the pass,' I said.

'Oh, the pass,' they said together. A pause.

'Can you take me?' I asked, feeling as though I was stating the obvious but uncertain if they hadn't stopped simply out of idle curiosity.

'Oh no,' said two voices, 'but you might as well get in.'

The invitation seemed to make perfect sense.

'We couldn't leave a young man walking up the road in this heat, could we?' said the driver.

'No, not walking up the road in this heat,' replied his accomplice, reassuring me in the process that they were in fact two separate people.

'We did it too many times when we were young,' he added.

'Oh yes, often we had to do it... when courting,' smiled the driver.

Through a series of couplets and echoes my conductors revealed themselves to be headed for the village midway to the pass. Their conversation turned left and right with the bends, and I empathised with their enthusiasm at returning to the mountains. They in turn commiserated with me for working in an office.

As we arrived in the village and the car drew up under a plane tree like a dog seeking shade, I thanked them profusely. They said 'think nothing of it' (together) and ushered me to the bar.

'Would you like a glass of beer?' asked the one with the sombrero;

'Of course he would,' said the one with the moustache.

Of course I did.

I learned of the broken ribs sustained by old Madame M. in a fall, and of the increasingly alcoholic tendencies of Monsieur P. Over the second glass I hear of the sombrero wearer's adventures in London, echoed by those of the moustachioed raconteur in Paris. I failed in my attempts to pay, though they admired my walking trousers that zipped off into shorts.

'Always clever, the English,' they said; 'Very practical,' they agreed.

The car was gently woken from its siesta, and I was once more conveyed up hill. After a couple of miles we stopped, as our paths were to separate.

'Only a few miles now,' they said.

'Enjoy your holiday - it's a beautiful area.'

I already knew they were right

Paul Howard, 31 years old, Journalist, England

Favourite Hobbies: Cycling, running and fell-walking, gardening

Favourite Country: Afghanistan

Favourite Book: The Outsider by Albert Camus

Other Publishing Experience: Riding High - Shadow Cycling the Tour de France and numerous articles

12 BIG TIGER

Bangkok. Shit. I wanted a story. And for my sins, I got one.

It took me a year to make the journey and, as I travelled slowly up the swollen, turbid length of the Chao Phraya river and saw the great prison rising up in front of me, I wondered. Did I still want the story?

The Thais call this place *Big Tiger*. It is a bestial place; they say Big Tiger 'prowls and eats.' It is the most notorious of the Thai prisons. Inside its walls are 8,000 of the killers and traffickers that the system caught. People confuse Big Tiger with the Bangkok Hilton. Believe me, the Thai jail Lard Jao really is the Hilton in comparison with this place. This is the boarding house with cardboard for walls and roaches for neighbours; the hotel with blood on the sheets.

There are no rules here. Men are in chains. Cruel, inhumane punishments are regular. The sewers are open and the air smells of shit. Water for drinking and washing comes straight from the Chao Phraya, downstream of the effluence pipe. TB and AIDS are spreading like wildfire. There are rats, roaches, lice and fleas. Homosexuality is frowned upon but the pigs on the pig farm get fucked by the inmates. Murders are frequent, guards are corrupt and embassies powerless. Welcome to Bang Kwang, where 8,000 lifers wait to die.

This is the place your Rough Guide won't take you. It is not marked on the map.

I was writing a screenplay and I needed to interview a heroin smuggler. After months of negotiation with the British Embassy in Bangkok I'd been given visiting orders to Bang Kwang.

I stepped off the boat and my resolve turned to dust, joining the dirt and spat tobacco around my feet. I was in a holding pen with a hundred others trying to get their V.O.s approved. Women collapsed to the ground, sobbing and screaming. The crowd around them pushed on, unmoved, edging closer to the desk where a row of uniformed prison officers sat. I handed over my visiting order. The officer took it, scanned it, pushed it back:

'Dead.'

Now the crying made sense. I learn that in this prison there are many deaths. I searched and found another order. I held it out. As the officer studied me, I felt cheap. Pick a card, any card. One dead - no problem. I got another right here.

He handed me a pass. I grabbed my bag and pushed against the tide out onto a dirt road, on the other side of which Big Tiger crouched, encased in razor wire, edged with gun towers, waiting, edgy, ready to spring. I was about to cross when a hand snatched out and grabbed my wrist. Towering above me was a man with a mouth of gold teeth. He watched me, took me in. He said hello and smiled, but I saw motive in his eyes and the grip on my arm felt like a trap. I shook him off and fled to Bang Kwang.

After the first set of vast gates I'm herded into the search area. Apparently in Bang Kwang I won't be needing anything. My bag is emptied in front of me. The carton of cigarettes I've brought comes under contraband. They're *put aside*. My guess is that it's going to be perfectly legal for the guards to smoke them later. The guard picks up my camera. He studies me, and turns the camera over.

'Why camera?'

In my bag there's a roll of Thai baht. Before I got here I had imagined bargaining my way through Thailand, where everyone has their price. But my western arrogance went the way of the fags and my all-persuasive American dollars. The money would go, but not in exchange for the safe passage of my camera.

'No camera. Understand? No camera.'

To make it clear he tore out my film and threw it into the brazier. I watched the celluloid twist and melt.

I'm shoved into the next enclosure, a dark hole of a room with a ceiling so far above me it merges with the darkness. This place is full of a damp cold. I'm led to another looming iron gate. This time a small door is cut into it. A guard slams back the bolt and shoves me through. The door pounds shut behind me.

They call this the Monkey House. Blinding sunshine and the smell of shit. It's bedlam. Cages like kennels run the length of the yard. Thai families herd around the bars on one side, and on the other the *farangs* or foreigners. The noise is insane: screaming and bellowing. And everywhere packs of guards pat their thick bamboo canes, watching, waiting.

I take up a place on the bleached bench and wait for my trafficker, and it's then I realise why everyone shouts. There are two sets of bars and a four-foot wide concrete trench separating us from the prisoners. We're all going to be shouting.

From behind the bars in the gloom men shuffle slowly past, their legs in chains. My mouth is dry. I'm here like carrion, gleaning information from the chained and the dying. And here comes my corpse, sweat-drenched and high-coloured, his skin loose on his body.

He tells me his story, about the girls and the money, about the super ego and the feeling of invincibility that led him to traffic hundreds of kilos of Thai White, the heroin that led him to Bang Kwang. He tells me about Big Tiger. The face of this man - who has been fighting since the day he could walk - shrinks with fear when he talks about Big Tiger. He tells me that Hell exists and it lies to the north of Bangkok. The men here will never go home. Here a life sentence is a hundred years.

I wanted a story. And for my sins, I got one.

Harriet Warner, 32 years old, Writer, England

Favourite Country: Italy

Favourite book: The Razor's Edge by W. Somerset Maugham

Other Publishing Experience: Features for various magazines and newspapers, two Episodes of Footballers' Wives, a pilot for a new ITV drama and an untitled screenplay & novel

13 WRONG PLANE!

I am the only jet-setting executive I know who has boarded the wrong plane not once, but twice. The fact that I was last employed thirteen years ago has nothing to do with my propensity to screw up business trips.

The first time I arrived at the airport late, a bad habit of mine. The last passenger to board the evening flight out, I squeezed into the middle seat and inanely commented to the businessman sitting next to me.

'Off to New Brunswick too, eh?'

He looked at me with alarm.

'I thought this flight was going to Newfoundland.'

'Uh-uh.' I shook my head sagely and showed him my boarding pass.

'*Saint John*, New Brunswick,' I said slowly as if talking to someone slightly retarded, 'Not *St. John's*, Newfoundland,' I added, emphasising the extra 's'.

He undid his seat belt and squeezed past me, opened the overhead luggage compartment, pulled out his coat and briefcase, and ran frantically to the front of the aircraft. I shook my head as he discussed his problem with the flight attendant.

The aircraft jolted as it was manoeuvred away from the terminal while the passenger returned down the aisle, calmly opened the baggage compartment overhead, replaced his coat and briefcase, squeezed past me, sat in his window seat, took his time doing up his safety belt, and then turned to me and hooked his thumb at his chest.

'I'm on the right aircraft. *You're* on the wrong one, and it's too late to get off buddy.'

I had no luggage in the hold, so no one cared. We flew *over* Saint John New Brunswick to Newfoundland, and no one gave a toss.

The second time was more serious, on an international flight from Montreal to London.

The fully-loaded jumbo jet was taxiing towards the apron when the pilot announced:

'Welcome on board Air Canada flight 417 to Paris…'

'Did he say… Paris?' I asked the woman sitting next to me.

'Oui,' she replied, acknowledging my presence with the distaste normally reserved for belching toads.

I pushed the flight attendant button. An irate stewardess strode down the aisle.

'Monsieur?' she enquired curtly, not brooking any nonsense.

'Ah… is this flight going to… Paris?'

This was not the time to practice my French.

'Oui.'

'But I'm going to London,' I stammered.

'Your boarding pass?' She flung out a hand.

I searched through my pockets eventually locating the boarding pass in the breast pocket of my shirt. This was before computerised boarding passes. She examined the stub and without saying a word, paced down the aisle towards the front. The luggage racks overhead creaked and groaned as we continued to bump towards the runway.

The stewardess came back a minute later followed by the purser.

'Hare you Handrew Stevenson?' he asked.

'Oui, I mean yes.'

'May Hi see your passport?'

I rummaged through several pockets before extracting my passport from a jacket.

'Hand this is *your* boarding card?'

'Yes.' Who else's would it be?

'Hand you hare going to *London*?'

'Yes.' That *is* what it says on my boarding card, I thought, regaining some composure.

''Ow did you get on this flight?'

'I don't know,' I pleaded.

I'm just a passenger. Look, someone checked my boarding

pass when I went through the gate in the terminal and someone else checked it before I boarded your aircraft. It's *your* job to stop idiots like me getting on the wrong aircraft so it's not *my* fault. All this I thought, but astutely and uncharacteristically kept my mouth shut. They both studied the boarding pass and then examined me, incredulous that this cretin, meaning me, had managed to board the wrong plane.

'Can Hi see your hairline ticket?' the purser demanded.

I rummaged around and found the ticket, which they both examined carefully. The aircraft continued taxiing. Two more flight attendants came to see what the commotion was about. I could feel curious passengers' eyes probing my row of seats.

'You 'ave baggage?' the purser confirmed, reaching out to show me the baggage reclamation receipt stuck onto the back of my ticket.

'A suitcase.'

That really stirred things up. The purser, with my air ticket, baggage identification and boarding card, jogged smartly down the aisle to the front, followed by the others. My hands were shaking so much I sat on them. For someone who has lived and travelled around the world several times, why do I have a propensity for getting myself into these situations?

Because I had luggage, and my suitcase, potentially full of bombs, was not on the same aircraft as me, I was a potential terrorist and a security risk.

The 747 juddered to a halt. We had just turned onto the runway. We remained there for what seemed like an eternity before, looking through the window, I saw a squad of Royal Canadian Mounted Police cars, lights flashing, approaching the aircraft. Minutes later a mobile staircase appeared. The flight attendants and purser congregated at the opened door and five burly RCMP officers boarded. Every passenger's eyes were on me as two burly police officers hauled me out by the armpits.

At the bottom of the staircase I was bundled into a police van and in a convoy of flashing lights and blaring sirens, hustled to another Air Canada 747, presumably the correct one, heading to London, with my baggage on board.

The mobile staircase nudged up to the second jumbo jet, and I was escorted up the stairs. The fuselage door opened, and I entered, showing my dog-eared boarding card to the purser. Sensing everyone's eyes on me again as I was led to the same seat but on the right aircraft, I acted with poise and dash: 007 on a last minute secret mission to save the world. But somehow, I don't think I pulled off the James Bond bit.

Austin Powers maybe. Mr Bean more likely.

Andrew Stevenson, Ageless, Male, Fulltime writer, Bermuda

Favourite Hobbies: Swimming, travelling, long-distance trekking, diving, triathlons, biking, running, kitesurfing, the list goes on

Favourite Country: Depends on the season, but New Zealand for sure, with Bhutan, Namibia, Norway, Argentina

Favourite Book: Constantly changes

Other Publishing Experience: Travels in Outback Australia as well as a number of other books

14 BY TRAIN ACROSS RAJASTHAN

Armed policemen from the 'tourist protection squad' passed along the First Class carriage. Apart from being shunted from one platform to another, the train had been sitting in Jaisalmer station for a couple of hours now.

A young girl from West Bengal, travelling with her family, had spoken to me briefly. Her father had also stopped for a word, and invited me to travel with the family, but I was content to sit on my own.

On my outward journey I had been disappointed that the desert was just miles and miles of flat scrub and sand, not the romantic image I had of undulating dunes patterned with stripes by unrelenting winds. But now and then the landscape was transformed by women working in the fields, saris in brilliant hues of red, orange, violet and gold, diaphanous veils held across their faces as they watched the train. In this impracticable garb they stooped to tend their crops. They carried heavy brass water pots on their heads with more poise than models on a catwalk.

Earlier the cook boy for the train had stopped to say hello. A pleasant, chatty boy of around fifteen, he had recognised me from my journey into Jaisalmer a few days previously. On that trip I shared a carriage with two women I had met in the hotel. I had qualms about them showing off all the gifts and mementoes they had bought, especially when they invited the cook boy to admire them.

The police checked right through the carriage and returned to the platform. The train jerked into motion. I sat back on the pale blue, plastic-covered thin layer of foam on the wooden bench seat, glad that I had an airpillow for a little comfort.

Three young men swung on to the end of the carriage as it finally crawled out of the station. I had seen them talking to the cook boy on the platform earlier. They obviously didn't have tickets for travelling First Class, if indeed they had tickets at all. They made straight for my compartment (I was the only Westerner on the train) and started chatting to me. One of them offered me biscuits from a packet. I declined. I had heard about Westerners being given drugged tea or food before being relieved of their valuables. They offered again, although they ate none themselves. I said I wasn't hungry. They became insistent. I refused again, politely. They became surly.

I sat in uncomfortable silence, my bags and rucksack under my seat. They were obviously discussing my luggage, and each time I looked up from studying the dusty, stained floor my gaze was met by three pairs of hostile eyes, the stares alternating between me and my baggage.

The journey seemed to be turning into a nightmare. I was relieved to catch sight of the Bengali girl in the corridor. Her family, very thoughtfully, had sent her to check on me so I asked if there was room for me to sit with them. I was even more relieved to gather up my belongings and join them. She and her younger brother were sitting with her mother and two aunts. Their three husbands were in the adjoining compartment, but even so they bolted the door from the corridor. Apart from the girl none of them spoke English, so conversation was limited, but I did not care a bit.

Susan Garrett Wright, 59 years old, Contemporary basketmaker, England

Favourite Hobbies: Listening to classical and world music, visual arts and traditional ethnic textiles

Favourite Country: Tibet

Favourite Book: Full Tilt on a Bicycle by Dervla Murphy

Other Publishing Experience: None

15 PUMPKIN SOUP

Most people have a foodstuff or drink, the very thought of which horrifies them. Apricot Schnapps was always mine. One night as a teenager did it for me and I can't even smell the stuff now without gagging. And then, of course, there's pumpkin...

In February 1990 three of us set off from a rainy Heathrow to start six months travelling, staying in an assortment of hostels and hovels. We did have a secret weapon though - one of us, Dan, was well connected. So occasionally we could step out of the world of the traveller into one of fresh linen, warm rooms and proper food!

Mid May we arrived in Auckland. We had spent the past month in Australia and were mere shells of the boys we once were. Poor food, late nights and copious amounts of alcohol left us in desperate need of home comforts. Once more, Dan to the rescue. His parents had some New Zealand friends. Partly to protect the guilty and partly because I can't recall their names let's call them John and Anne.

The first signs were good as we were met at the airport by Anne. When we arrived at the house, we were stunned. A large drive led to an imposing five bedroom town house. The front door opened into a regency-style hall complete with three-tiered staircase running around the outside of the room. The hall was completed by an enormous chandelier, priceless looking paintings and beautiful furniture.

We freshened up in our en suite bathroom. After an hour or so we all met up in the family kitchen, the smell of fresh food thick in the air. John explained that unfortunately they had to go out that evening. Anne brought out our dinner - pumpkin soup for starters. The soup was a thick sludge of fluorescent orange; not my favourite but it tasted okay.

Of course we all fell into that age-old trap, of wanting to make a good impression:

'Anne, this soup is absolutely delicious. Thank you so much!'

'Would you like some more, boys?'

'Erm, ok then...'

Not so chirpy now. Three bowls later we were greeted by a main course of sausages and peas. Two further helpings later we were virtually comatose. John and Anne left the house for the night.

What follows is not for sensitive readers.

We decided that TV and some beers would be the best plan. About thirty minutes in Dan literally exploded out of his chair and dashed out into the hall. We were greeted with the sounds of someone being sick; Dan was greeted with laughter. Ten minutes later the same happened to Ed. I was feeling okay - a bit full and, as I hadn't thrown up, full of myself. It all changed very suddenly.

I was lounging on the sofa when the first gag reflex hit me. I sat up immediately and a second came - this time containing a small amount of warm liquid. I calmly stood up and walked towards the hall. I'd just about made it when my mouth filled up with a sickly sweet tasting mixture of pumpkin soup, sausage gristle and peas. That's when it suddenly hit me that I had no idea where the downstairs toilet was.

I could feel the next gag coming and I was in no position to shout through to Ed and Dan for directions. The only toilet I knew was in our room so I broke into a run up the staircase. As I hit the second flight of stairs my fourth gag arrived and with it enough sick to completely fill my mouth. I now broke into a sprint.

Just as I rounded the top of the stairs onto the landing the inevitable happened. The force of the vomit, my already full mouth and the centrifugal force of my sprint conspired to give a huge amount of sick a huge amount of propulsion. It went everywhere - imagine Monty Python's Mr Creosote. After the first proper vomit I delivered another four straight off. Nature had taken over and I was powerless even to move.

Dan and Ed rushed into the hall, drawn by what they imagined were several sizeable gas explosions, to be greeted by a scene of utter devastation. The staircase, banister, carpet and walls were covered in a bright orange paste, the monotony of which was occasionally broken up by a lump of sausage meat or the odd pea. Three expensive looking pictures had dashes of bright orange that probably weren't part of the artist's original vision.

Antique tables were covered in a thin orange sheen. A large basket of laundered white clothes which sat on the landing now looked in need of several more washes. And the *pièce de resistance* was a large stringy piece of orange mucus hanging down from the chandelier. We all stood there as orange slowly oozed and I could only just mutter 'F#%@!' before I finally found the upstairs toilet to heave once again.

The clear up operation took a full two hours, including time off for further heavings. We discussed upping and leaving to hide in Auckland but Dan thought this might strain his parents' friendship. The laundry was hand washed and put in the drier, the pictures were delicately restored to their original state and an elaborate cloth on the end of a broom saw to the chandelier. Windows were opened and deodorant sprays tested as never before.

As the last trace was mopped up we heard a car in the drive. As the door opened I double checked the surroundings all looked clear. Just to be sure I picked up the phone - the receiver was covered in vomit. A quick final wipe and I went downstairs to welcome our genial hosts

We stayed another five days, and nothing was ever said. Whether our hosts ever knew about that night we don't know I guess they do now. I have not managed to look at a pumpkin since.

Duff Battye, 33 years old, Musician, England

Favourite Hobbies: Motorbike racing, scuba diving, climbing, history

Favourite Country: Wales

Favourite Book: Flashman and the Great Game by George MacDonald Fraser

Other Publishing Experience: None

16 BORDER LUNACY

The full moon was rising over Laos on the far bank of the Mekong, its reflection glimmering on the surface of the slow-moving river. The food was acceptable and the conversation amusing. Somewhere in the dark the sound of fireworks seemed to be occurring with increasing frequency. The Chinese New Year had already occurred in Thailand but gangs of little boys seemed to be continuing the celebrations.

A thumping sound drummed a worrying beat in my mind and made me silence my companions.

'Listen...'

Silence reigned

'What the...?'

'Listen....'

A 'bup-bup-bup' sound cut the stillness, and repeated. The answer was dawning on me.

'It sounds like a...' I began, but at that moment a brilliant light blossomed in the sky. The word 'Kalashnikov' died on my lips. We stared, hypnotised, as the parachute flare slowly descended. The shadows crossed our faces as it swung down, and I realised that we were brightly illuminated and framed in the window, making a perfect target by the light of the flare. Suddenly everything erupted; the fast ripping sound of a couple of machine guns sent two pretty but deadly streams of tracer bullets intertwining in the air, up from the Laotian side, echoed by several other guns. I leaned over and went to the floor, away from the window, my heart pounding

'Get down, they're shooting!' I yelled and they goggled at me crouched like a fool on the floor.

Still crouching I went out the back door into the street at a run, quickly followed by Sharon and Dave. The restaurant staff were already huddled below the stairs. Which side of the river the gunfire and flares came from it was now hard to tell, but if the big one was on between Laos and Thailand then we were going to be caught right in the middle. We were very frightened.

A Thai border police post was across the road and the door of the first floor opened, throwing a shaft of light into the street and silhouetting a policeman on the verandah with an M16. He snapped the bolt back and opened fire. I couldn't be sure in the confusion, but he did seem to be aiming a bit high. We blocked our ears until the brief fusillade was over, and then another policeman at ground level cut loose with a submachine gun, tearing through a full magazine in a couple of seconds. I turned in the direction they seemed to be shooting and saw that the sky was suddenly very dark, as if the moon had been covered by a giant hand.

The penny dropped. A lunar eclipse was occurring, and the shooting, I realised belatedly but with great relief, was to frighten off the evil spirits which caused it.

The firing stopped as it became completely dark for maybe ten minutes, and I could hear people coming out into the street. As the moon's light appeared on the other side of the black shadow, a further jubilant burst of firing celebrated the defeat of the bad spirits, but it quickly dwindled to single shots. Most of the ammunition had been expended too freely already by our trigger-happy defenders. The lunacy was over.

Steve Kelleher, 37 years old, Australian government, but always on leave, Australia

Favourite Hobbies: Bushwalking, reading, sleeping, boomerang throwing

Favourite Country: Laos

Favourite Book: One Crowded Hour by Tim Bowden

Other Publishing Experience: Some in-house articles and a few paragraphs in Lonely Planet newsletters

17 DOORWAY TO DISEASE

'Don't let there be blood. Please don't let there be blood.'

I held my breath, looked down; there was blood.

'Bitch!'

My head, echoing the desperate beat of a panicking heart, found it impossible to comprehend. I tried to calm myself and think. Guidebooks say that when bitten by a rabid animal one should clean the wound immediately and get straight to hospital. I didn't know if this dog was to be the carrier for my very own hydrophobic nightmare, but I wasn't going to take any chances.

Cleansing the wound as best I could with dregs from my water bottle, I squeezed to try to remove excess bacteria from this newly formed doorway to disease.

Salvation or salivation? I quickly headed to the ubiquitous vendors, where I attempted to express my fears.

'*Sawadee kha*,' I offered the first vendor. She looked at me, a bored expression on her face, waiting listlessly for my choice of beverage. I had just uttered the extent of my Thai, so continued,

'English, do you speak English?' No reply.

'Please, do you speak English?' No reply.

'I've just been bitten by a dog. I need hospital, please. RABIES!'

I pointed to the blood trickling down my leg hoping this would initiate some response - it didn't. Floundering somewhat, all the while knowing time was of the essence, I now began to bark! Quietly at first, then with more aggression. Pointing to my leg with one hand and waggling the fingers of the other over my mouth, I pathetically attempted to mime rabid foam. At the sight of this lunatic Englishman behaving like a freak in front of her, she turned and ran into the shop behind. I couldn't blame her.

A moment later she returned, an angry looking man accompanying her. Thinking that a swift lesson in Thai boxing was about to ensue, I held up my hands and pleaded:

'Help.'

'What you want?' he barked.

'You speak English. Thank God!'

The poor lady's husband, Selee, told me the dog was wild and had been wandering the ruins for the last week. It had been hostile towards other tourists but had not, to his knowledge, bitten anyone else. Great. The privilege was mine.

The fact remained that I needed to get to hospital quickly and Selee offered to take me in his truck. The day was getting hotter and as the truck bumped and shimmied along the road that would take us to the centre of Ayuthaya, I closed my eyes and thought back.

An hour earlier I was in my element. I'd hired a bike from my hostel, which despite first impressions was doing a marvellous job of transporting me around the former Thai capital. The morning sun was glorious and I had even managed to find my way to the first three temples on my tour, despite the most misleading of maps.

It was at Wat Phra Mahathat that it all went pear-shaped.

I'd finished wandering around this impressive ruin, taken arty photos of Buddha torsos, admired the precariously supported *prangs* and *chedis* and was returning fondly to my bike when bounding frivolity caught my eye. Behind me a pack of half a dozen of the cutest puppies were engaged in fun and frolic. Now, I don't consider myself 'soppy' in any way, but I challenge anyone not to have been moved by the playful adventures of these tail-wagging bundles of fluff.

Grabbing my camera I crept forward and snapped a couple of shots. Smiling to myself I turned to go and was confronted by a look of pure rage. Before me stood the bitch mother, quivering lips pulled back over yellow teeth, black eyes staring at me filled with territorial aggression.

I knew that, throughout Asia, when it came to an aggressive dog the accepted practice was to throw a well-aimed stone. If no suitable rock were near, then allegedly a theatrical bluff would produce the desired, cowering canine effect. But as this was running through my mind the dog suddenly barked, sprang toward me and sank its jaws into my calf. Seemingly satisfied that any threat to her offspring had been (literally) nipped in the bud, she then padded past me, back to her pups.

At Ayuthayas medical centre, Selee explained my predicament. After a lengthy wait I was ushered into a sterile room and patient met doctor, who smiled radiantly. He seemed excessively amused by my fear of rabies, nodding a great deal, like a cheeky marionette, and filling the room with hearty laughter. I was informed there was no way of knowing unless the dog was caught, killed and tested. If the dog was infected, it would soon show signs and expire in dramatic fashion. Was this to be our shared fate? My foresight in obtaining a costly set of vaccinations before arriving in Thailand was slight comfort. A booster was given and the wound cleaned.

Selee drove me back to the site and gave me his details. I was to call in two weeks to see how the dog was. I thanked him, and as he hugged me goodbye I thought what an amazing part of travel was the kindness shown by total strangers. I threw my newly bandaged leg over my bike and pedalled away. In the distance, near one of the ruins, my attacker shepherded her pack around a corner and was gone.

Of course the dog never had rabies. I spent the next weeks worrying that I would start to fear water and then go mad - it never happened. After trekking in Chang Mai, I gave Selee a call. Happily, he told me that the dog was around and healthy. I still bear the scar, and keep my vaccination card as a reminder. It has a simple drawing in the corner; the black outlined head of a happy dog shadowed by the red one of a snarling beast. I wonder how many other tourists have the same memento of a mother's love.

Marc Witkowski, 36 years old, Telesales, England

Favourite Hobbies: Travel, tennis, live role playing

Favourite Country: South America, if I had to choose it would be Peru

Favourite Book: Endurance by Alfred Lansing

Other Publishing Experience: None

18 LAST TAKE-OFF FROM BAGHDAD

It was the day of the World Cup Final. The Airbus arrived from Bahrain and I went up to the cockpit to have a coffee with them. It was the Captain's last flight for a spell as he was returning home for some overdue leave. I wished him a safe flight back.

The plane taxied down the runway. Before seeking a TV to watch the big match I wandered out to watch the take-off. The pilots had been doing some spectacular flying lately and Eric, the Captain, got the Airbus off the deck in the first quarter of the runway then performed an elegant steep bank past the tower before heading homewards.

I was about to board the jeep when a huge cloud of smoke billowed from the disappearing Airbus which began to lose height immediately, smoke streaming from the port wing. I prayed it was some sort of engine failure, but deep down I knew it had been hit by a missile. I rang the tower to find out if they could speak to the pilots. As we spoke I watched in horror as flame shot out of the wing.

Eric reported he could see nothing, but he heard a huge bang and lost all hydraulics. To the uninitiated this meant he was unable to use his wing flaps, tail flaps or ultimately his brakes. Try and imagine that you are driving down the motorway in the fast lane, and your steering wheel and brakes fail. But you have some capacity to steer because you have two accelerators that control respectively the speed of your nearside and offside wheels. In the case of the plane you also have gravity to contend with.

Watching, I could see clearly that Eric was struggling to control the aircraft and trying to lose height, rather too successfully at first. Thankfully he leveled out, but as he did so a huge flame swept the length of the aeroplane as the wingtip fuel tank ignited. Dreadful images of the Columbia space shuttle flashed through my mind, but by a miracle the fuel caused no further explosion.

For the next twenty minutes Eric nursed the plane around in a circuit, getting lower and lower as he used the power of first one engine and then the other to steer the plane in a downwards spiral. Everything seemed to be happening in slow motion. I was trying desperately to think of extra ways to help, but the only things to be done were to ensure all the emergency services were ready and that Head Office knew what was happening ahead of the reporters.

I also made sure the employees stayed calm, as the increasingly excited Iraqis threatened to crank up the tension. My concern was that this could cause errors on the ground and we could then have two problems on our hands. I kept one eye on the plane and the other on the staff.

After what seemed a month the crew managed to bring the plane back towards the airport and now they were going to be faced with the task of landing without brakes or flaps. Eric was clearly going for the military side of the airport, where there were less obstacles close to the runway. At this point all the Iraqis rushed to the vehicles, clearly bent on crossing the airport to be closer to the landing. I made them get out and hand over all the keys. The last thing we needed at this moment was forty hysterical staff driving round the airport at breakneck speed.

I jumped into the jeep and drove round myself to watch Eric land. The aircraft veered from one side to the other as he juggled his engines to straighten the approach. He was going too fast and was still a good fifty feet up crossing the fence. He chopped the throttles and the plane dropped out of the sky almost vertically, landing with a crash and a billow of smoke and dust. He used reverse thrust to slow down a little, but when he slewed towards the parked helicopters he over-compensated and went off the other side of the runway. The Airbus hit the sand, which helped slow it down and also helped to douse the flames still pouring from the wing. To get the plane down in one piece was a fine piece of flying.

I watched the escape slides pop out of the exits. There was none of the orderly removal of shoes and crossing of arms that you see in the manuals, these guys were running down the escape slides as they evacuated. At the same time the emergency crews, who had arrived almost instantaneously, started spraying the wing. Before they knew it, Eric, Steve and Mario were surrounded by the fire crew who were congratulating them, and already the crowds were crossing the runway.

The Airbus crew began to show the classic symptoms of shock: Steve and Mario were like rabbits caught in headlights, and Eric was dancing with joy, high on adrenalin. I pushed through the crowd, embraced all three of them at once, then led them away from the rapidly expanding throng. The initial comments from Eric and Mario were: 'the bastards shot us down,' and Steve just said: 'I'm twenty-nine years old and I've just used up all my luck.'

We took them over to the hospital for preliminary checks and they all seemed physically fine, though emotionally as high as kites which was natural and normal. Rather than let them settle down we headed back to the plane to ensure they had completed the close-down procedures, and to pick up their documents and effects. There was also time to inspect the damage and to pose for photos. On returning to the plane the military had already cordoned the area off. I was glad they had reacted so quickly. The media were already hot on the trail, and tomorrow's headlines would say the score was one-nil to Iraq.

Heyrick Bond Gunning, 32 years old, Consultant, Iraq

Favourite Hobbies: Sport, writing, travel, marathons

Favourite Country: UK

Favourite Book: The English Patient

Other Publishing Experience: Baghdad Business School is being published in September

19 A NEAR RUN THING

I flew into Brussels at mid-day with a guilty secret and a troubled conscience.

There was in those days a thriving Scots community in the Belgian capital, who shared a common problem. Apparently all their British visitors, even before unpacking, would start asking about the Duke of Wellington and the Battle of Waterloo. In those early years of the EEC Brussels had no other associations for Brits, not even chocolate or fruit beers. As some wag pointed out, all Scots carried a picture of the Duke close to their hearts - but that was before His Grace was ousted from the back of the £5 note in favour of Elizabeth Fry.

Unfortunately, the hospitable hosts knew absolutely nothing about the Duke or the battle. Some-one mentioned this problem to his 'bother-in-law' (a Freudian slip?), who swiftly arranged for me to be invited over to lecture to them, so that in future they could answer their guests' questions with confident authority.

Initially, this was fine by me. I had been a military history fanatic for twenty years, my special interest was the Napoleonic Wars, and my hero was Wellington. For years I had mugged up every detail of all his victories from Assaye to Waterloo, which last was the one I knew and loved best. Also, I was far from averse to the sound of my own voice. So my only decision was not what to say, but what to omit.

Finally, my confidence levels had recently been topped-up by a smashing letter from Elizabeth, Lady Longford, who thanked me charmingly for pointing out three tiny errors of detail in her highly successful book *Wellington - Years of the Sword*. She also listed the distinguished experts who hadn't spotted those errors at proof stage but now acknowledged them, no doubt through gritted teeth.

With all this going for me, you would think my only worry would be that the Belgian doorways wouldn't be wide enough to admit my swollen head.

Which brings me to my guilty secret: I had never actually been to Waterloo. All the rest - Talavera, Ciudad Rodrigo, Salamanca, the lot. But for some reason, not Waterloo. You could argue that with ample second-hand knowledge I would be fine, but daily I grew less and less convinced. One awkward question, from someone who knew that ominously local terrain, and I would stand exposed, my credibility completely destroyed.

It would be like the pilot saying to the passengers: 'No, I haven't actually flown an aeroplane before, but it's quite all right, because I've studied all the manuals carefully *and* done the correspondence course.' The old and frail would be trampled to death in the rush for the exit.

But I could see no alternative to taking my chances. One thing in my favour was that if many of my audience really knew their stuff, it was highly unlikely they would have voted for bringing in an outside expert. I sought comfort from one of my favourite authorities: Harvard Professor Tom Lehrer said (or rather, sang): 'Plagiarize, plagiarize, let no one else's work evade your eyes.' Good, uplifting advice, but I was still very nervous.

It was only after landing and booking into my hotel room that a possible (but hopelessly belated) solution dawned. It was still early afternoon. My lecture was next morning. How long would it take to get from Brussels to Waterloo? Might I race round the battlefield before dark, and thus plug the fatal gap in my qualifications?

A long shot Watson, but the game was afoot - and so was I. I'll spare you the details but I made it, in the nick of time.

I ignored the little village of Mont St. Jean with its tacky souvenir shops, and as the area emptied and the sun sank I made for high ground. I spurned the oversized Lion memorial, a vulgar and undeserved tribute to the inept Prince William of Orange and his equally useless Army Corps (many of whom had deserted rather than fight). Instead I headed for Wellington's command post, no longer marked by his famous elm tree.

My best vantage point was the nearby memorial to Colonel Alexander Gordon, whose death at the battle's end triggered Wellington's first tears. It is an obelisk on a raised dais, reached via a short flight of stone steps rising directly from the main Brussels-Genappe road, which runs North-South and neatly bisects Wellington's lines.

From there I had a magnificent view of the entire battlefield. I stood for twenty minutes as the shadows deepened, re-appraising each phase of the battle in its real-life setting. The struggle to hold Hougoumont, in the hollow away to my right; d'Erlon's attack on Picton's Division to my left front; Ney's repeated cavalry charges, broken against the British squares; the bloody contest for La Haye Sainte farmhouse (rebuilt and pristine directly below me); the crisis point, with Napoleon's Old Guard marching up the slope to my right, to be thrown back as never before, just as the Prussians swept in from my extreme left to turn the French setback into a rout.

With 44,000 dead and wounded, spread over three square miles.

I shivered and turned away reluctantly, to descend the steps. My foot slipped, just as I saw and heard the vast *camion* approaching fast on my side of the road, heading for Genappe. As my slip became a stumble, my balance went. I slithered and fell, down the steep steps heading straight for the path of the hurtling juggernaut. Everything went into slow motion. Scrabbling frantically to recover, clutching for the iron handrail, I had time to think:

'My God, this is it!'

And then, crazily, in what must surely be my last second of life, I knew exactly what I wanted on my headstone. No one could ask for better:

'He fell at Waterloo.'

I felt the blast of the slipstream. I will never know how I survived.

But it made a good ending for my lecture.

Cowan Third, 59 years old, Management consultant, Scotland

Favourite Hobbies: Military history, golf

Favourite Country: Spain

Favourite Book:1809 Army List

Other Publishing Experience: Many articles & a few short stories

20 BOREDOM: THE GREAT ESCAPE

I may have mentioned how I got this great deal, by which in return for house- and cat-sitting I get a free month in June, Florida and the lap of luxury. Florida, where good American ladies go to dye their hair. Mostly purple.

Or so I'm told. Because the truth is I didn't see any good American ladies. Worse, I didn't see any bad ones either. The entire population of Port St. Lucie was always where I wasn't. After three days I was bored out of my skull, and desperate as poor Ben Gunn for some human companionship. Until a friend rang from England.

'You should come over, it's amazing,' I assured him, trying to sound convincing. Trying to keep the note of sheer desperation out of my voice:

'Beautiful weather, great bars, gorgeous chicks everywhere wearing nothing but designer bikinis and rollerblades. I promise.'

He came over, and within a day he was calling me a liar.

Within two days he was looking seriously depressed.

'Look!' I said. We were walking along the magical Hobe Sound. Just the two of us.

'Ospreys!'

It didn't help. Next day he caught a plane to Cuba, and I started having long conversations with the cat.

Then I met Angie. She saved my life. She wasn't American, which maybe helped. She was Canadian. Aged around fifty, tough and laconic like a character by Annie Proulx. Husband in the state pen for holding up a pharmacy. He'd got addicted to morphine-based painkillers.

'Poor guy,' I said.

'Asshole,' she said.

I liked Angie a lot.

'Yeah,' she said, 'Port St. Lucie is kinda draggy. Tell you what. I'll take you fishing.'

We drove out past the endless strip malls, the suburbs-without-a-centre and along US Highway 1, then we turned off down a back road and eventually came to something almost resembling the wilds. We parked under some pine trees, Angie got a net from the back of the car and waded into the nearby muddy creek looking for livebait.

'What about alligators?' I asked anxiously, rolling up my trouser-legs.

She ignored me for a while, scooping around with her net. Then she said:

'It's not the alligators that'll eat you, it's the mosquitoes. And the no-see-ums.'

'No-see-ums?' Even more anxious.

'Yeah,' she drawled, 'Because you'll no-see-um. You'll feel 'em, though. Bite hurts like hell.'

'I've got some repellent somewhere,' I said, and she shrugged:

'No point. You'll get bit anyhow.'

And we got bit. And it hurt like hell. But it didn't seem to matter, somehow. Once we'd got a bucketful of livebait we drove down to the shores of the Indian River, hooked them up and started to fish. There was no one else around. The sun was going down behind us over Florida, over the Gulf and beyond that over the mountains of Mexico. We had a couple of beers each and Angie rolled a spliff and we smoked.

The water in front of us darkened, and it was getting almost too late to fish. Then we caught a single snook, which you can just about eat if you don't mind a lot of bones. But at least we'd caught it ourselves, and it didn't come already dusted with Cajun-Style Spices and topped with Cheddar-Style Cheese. So we found some dried-out driftwood, started a fire at the river's edge, grilled our snook and we ate it. A very Huck Finn moment.

And then the sun was gone and the air was very still and quiet, and out on the miles-wide Indian River a white ship went past us in the darkness not making a sound.

For my last week, Angie said I should go down to Key West.
'Now that's a fun place.'

I was wary.

'It's…I mean, it's quite gay, no?'

'Yeah, there's a lot of gays down there. But you'll be OK, they'll never hit on you.'

'What d'you mean? Why not?' I felt quite indignant. (There's no pleasing some people.)

'It's…' She scrutinized me. 'I guess it's the way you English guys dress.'

I looked down. I was wearing my beloved Clarks Jesus sandals with the air-cushion soles; my father's old but still mostly white tennis shorts, circa 1947; and an only slightly sweat-stained T-shirt advertising the Bear Inn in Bisley, Glos.

I couldn't see what she was talking about.

'No, you'll be fine in Key West,' she said, 'Really.'

She was right. I loved Key West.

In Key West in the summer, the ripe mangoes fall from people's trees in their gardens, and they pick them up and leave them out on their garden walls for passers-by just to help themselves.

In Key West, almost everyone walks or cycles. The streets are too old and narrow for cars. But if you walk or cycle, you do so slowly. So you can stop and chat to other people passing by.

In Key West, old sea-dogs with grizzled beards really do sit down by the harbourside, swigging white Cuban rum from the bottle and talking about the size of the tarpon or the shark that got away.

In Key West, everyone gathers in Mallory Square every evening to watch the sunset, which they say is probably the best in the world. And as the sun goes down you get people fire-eating, and doing card tricks, and selling ice-cold margaritas from little hand-barrows, and there's a dog who wears a red spotted hanky round his neck and walks the length of a tightrope wagging his tail furiously the whole time so you wonder how on earth he can stay on.

In 1982, Key West officially seceded from the Union and declared itself an Independent Republic. They then declared war on the

United States. Five minutes later they offered an unconditional surrender, in return for $1 million of 'foreign' aid.

Washington didn't get the joke. Key West didn't get the money.

But in Key West, people say they're not in America. They're in Key West.

Maybe that was why I liked it.

Christopher Hart, 38 years old, Novelist and journalist, England

Favourite Hobbies: Hiking, travel, painting

Favourite Country: Ireland

Favourite Book: Moby Dick by Herman Melville

Other Publishing Experience: Various travel articles for newspapers. Three novels - The Harvest, Rescue Me and Julia

21 ROAD RAGE IN ISTANBUL

Last summer, during a four month road trip spent rambling through Europe, we got plenty of opportunities to fine tune the art of staying alive on the roads: no mean feat in some of the places we found ourselves.

But without a doubt the biscuit goes to Istanbul.

Although of the cities we visited it was one of my favourites, the roads were 'an experience', and after accomplishing the gauntlet that is Istanbul I can safely say I could drive anywhere.

Just getting into the city in the blistering heat took us several hours - us and what felt like the rest of Turkey. Admittedly, we were lost, but this wasn't helped by the fact that, apparently without cause or reason, a perfectly normal two lanes of flowing traffic would suddenly morph into a five lane beast of terror.

In the beginning we were powerless and could only watch as our hard-found exit point slowly grew nearer and nearer...so close, only to be physically shunted further away by hell-bent drivers as they beetled in and out and around, incessantly honking and waving. I don't know how many times we found that exit only to watch glumly as it receded once more into the distance. Four hours we had of this, I swear. Tempers were becoming frayed.

Finally we stopped, exhausted, ambushed a yellow taxi driver and pleaded with him to let us follow him to our destination. There followed a breakneck chase through the city with us barely keeping up with our guide, who seemed intent on shaking us. And we hadn't even paid him yet. He was racing ahead, chopping lanes, creating new ones, cutting people up, not indicating, braking then careering across junctions. And there were yellow taxis everywhere. Apparently Istanbul has 60,000 and I think we saw them all.

At every enforced standstill, when the volume of traffic inhibited even the Kamikaze, our crazy guide would cheerfully wave to us in his mirror.

By the end I was driving in the manner of the locals, breaking every conceivable highway code along with the best of them.

Then the car battering occurred.

A driver behind us, perhaps distracted by the sight of a British car driven by girls and loaded with what appeared to be smalls (Claire's laundry spread out to dry in the back, possibly not our brightest move), careered into the back end of us. We had just discovered, to our eternal shame, that our car insurance didn't cover us in these parts. So we decided not to make a fuss. I smiled and made what I hoped were 'don't worry about it' gestures.

But no! This guy was fuming. He banged on our window, spitting bits of possible kebab in fury. He pointed to his bumper and made unmistakable gestures indicating it was our fault. The gist of his message appeared to be that we had reversed into him and therefore must pay. Calmly denying this version of events did little to help however and, as our taxi man was once again on the move, we did what any other conscientious, self-respecting foreign traveller would do. We stepped on it, in grand fashion.

The guy went crazy. We followed our yellow taxi, followed in turn by our new friend. He drove like a maniac all around us, gesturing wildly and trying to make us pull over. Although alarmed, we ignored him and even managed to feign indifference by turning up our one tape that worked and singing along in a carefree fashion. Claire even produced a nail file and made a big show of looking casual.

This incensed our pursuer even further, until his increasingly erratic driving was brought to an abrupt end as a result of cutting up one fellow Turk too many. As we at last reached our destination, he got shunted three lanes to the left and that was the end of that.

We waved goodbye to him to show no hard feelings.

Lucia Hunter, 28 years old, Midwife, England

Favourite Country: Europe as a whole as it is all so diverse

Favourite Book: Kate Adie's Kindness of Strangers

Other Publishing Experience: None

22 BAGGAGE PARTY

From behind the biggest moustache in East Africa, Roger - Officer Commanding 'A' Company - addressed his officers and senior NCOs in Company Office, his brick-red, sweating face beaming with suppressed excitement:

'Next week we move from Hargeisa to Mogadishu in Somalia. The Battalion travels by troopship, but we take the heavy baggage overland in ten-ton diesel lorries. It's about 600 miles, mostly unmade roads. It could take three days. When we cross the Ogaden the *shifta* may be after our stores, especially our weapons.

'Briefing to-morrow, but if we lose one round of ammunition this trip I'll have someone's guts for bloody garters, as the Colonel will have mine.'

As a raw, recently-joined subaltern I was more nervous of Roger's prospective wrath than of the abstract idea of Ethiopian bandits.

The first night we camped between Jijiga and Awareh. By mid-morning we were deep in the Ogaden savannah - scattered acacia thorns and six-foot-high anthills, under a sun so scalding that touching the lorry's metalwork raised blisters.

Engine noise plus language barrier limited communication with the stocky, nut-brown Italian driver. Nothing to do as we lurched along the rutted tracks but scan the endless bush for *shifta*, who were equipped (apparently) with firearms jettisoned by the retreating Italians seven years before, in '41. All I saw were a few tiny dik-dik.

Mine was the convoy's rear vehicle, with my platoon in the back, fully armed and issued with live ammunition. Peter, the senior subaltern, was riding point with his platoon in the front vehicle. Roger and the Company Sergeant Major drove in a jeep in mid-column, whilst the third platoon was split up amongst the remaining lorries, three or four men per vehicle, all armed. My orders were simple: keep station. If I hear shooting we head for the sound of the guns. The notion of armed bandits began to feel slightly less abstract.

Suddenly my driver wrenched at the wheel, pumping the footbrake as we heeled over to avoid a stationary vehicle directly ahead. I saw bush-hatted soldiers on the track. Ours.

'Fermata! Non guidare piu!' I think what I shouted meant 'Bus-stop!' but he braked hard.

The lorry in front had broken down. My orders were to stay at the back. Did this mean behind the last vehicle, or the main body? Dropping behind the convoy we'd be tactically useless. But could I abandon four soldiers, not to mention a loaded truck-and-trailer? Neither course of action sounded right. Which should I choose?

The driver indicated he could fix the engine.

'É securo?' I asked. He fluttered his hand horizontally. Not reassuring.

In the end I compromised, ordering Sergeant Lewis to take our lorry, plus platoon, catch up with the convoy and take station as rearguard. I would stay with the breakdown and its guardians, one of whom had a Bren-gun. Technically I had disobeyed orders, but I felt sure an officer should stay and share his men's fate, be it boredom, hardship or danger.

A quick check on the water situation - five full water-bottles, plus a couple of giant rope-covered ex-Chianti flasks - then we watched, thoughtfully, as our link with the outside world drove off in a dust cloud leaving us alone in the vast, hostile bush.

We *should* be okay. If the *shifta* didn't arrive; if the driver fixed the engine; if we didn't run out of water. Pretty big ifs.

The driver, shining with sweat in oil-stained green singlet, shorts and Somali sandals, worked non-stop. I sited the Bren-gun (on the trailer top for all-round fire) and posted sentries. Then we tried to find shade, cleaned and re-loaded our weapons, dozed fitfully, sipped disinfected water and ate tinned corned beef, of which we had a vast supply.

I felt fairly useless. Zero experience of this kind of soldiering, knowing nothing of the lads looking to me for leadership, *or* desert survival, *or* the internal combustion engine. Three hours later I gazed hopelessly at about a hundred separate engine parts spread out on groundsheets. Surely to God no one could put that lot together again in the right order, then just swing the starting handle?

I tried to project confidence, but inwardly I agonised. How to defend against a *shifta* attack? What if the engine defeated Luigi? Did we walk (which way?), or just sit and wait for passing traffic (if any)? Will they send someone back for us? When will the water run out? Was my tiny force getting restless?

The weight of responsibility eased massively at dawn next morning when the reassembled engine fired first time.

We set off, travelling fast. Would our repair hold? Could we catch the convoy? We had seen no *shifta*, but had they? Fresh questions to recycle constantly as we chased through the day and into the following night, only stopping when we had to, to flex stiffened muscles and re-fuel from the slung drums. Luigi seemed tireless.

The convoy was moving slowly. They had spent the second night at Wardair. At 2230 hours on the third night we caught up with them at Belet Wen, just over the Somalia border. Now on the fast, straight Italian road, we were only hours from Mogadishu.

They were safely laagered beside a King's African Rifles detachment. When I'd seen my little squad in good hands I made for the K.A.R. Officer's Mess, drawn there by the sound of raucous singing.

I was exhausted, filthy, unshaven, my khaki drill crumpled and sweat-stained. How would I be received? With congratulations, or open arrest? I found Roger leading a round-the-camp-fire rendition of *'The Good Ship Venus'*, beating time with his beer mug. I reported to him between verses. He swigged some Tusker, nodded at me and said cheerfully:

'Hello Jamie, where the hell have you been?'

Then, without waiting for my answer, he carried on singing:

> *'The Captain's wife was Mabel,*
> *She did all that she was able*
> *To fornicate with the Second Mate*
> *Upon the chartroom table!'*

Had our absence passed entirely un-noticed?

James Alexander, 75 years old, retired wine merchant, Italy

Favourite Hobbies: Tuscany, Italian Wine

Favourite Country: Italy

Favourite Book: Pride & Prejudice

Other Publishing Experience: None

23 SIKH AND YOU SHALL FIND

A sapphire blue turbaned head emerges from the lapis lazuli lake. Water drops drip down his dark leathered face, reflecting the light from the Golden Temple, then fall like diamonds back into the water of the night pool.

The man is a Sikh, a man of God, and a warrior. My eyes follow him as he takes his ritual evening bath in the holy, healing waters of the temple. He has a lifetime of crystal white hair reaching from his chin and beneath the fabric wrapped around his head. Nearby lie his crumpled cotton garments, laid out on the marble shore steps with the small decorative knife traditionally worn over a Sikh's shoulder.

Behind the Sikh's skeletal silhouette the monument of worship is centred perfectly, seeming to float on its own golden reflection amidst the dark waters of the lake. I am captivated by the allure of its mystical, magical and sacred devotion. Drifting in the hot night air Bejans - songs of prayer - come from within the heart of the glistening Golden Temple, which is built from tones of intricately carved gold. It is a haven protected within walls of white marble.

I am presently spending time with Manu, and we are together venturing to the Golden Temple in the city of Amritsar. Manu lives in Dharamsala in northern India, where I have been living for the past three months, and we have taken two days away from the cool mountains to travel down into the intense summer heat of the north west of India. This is mostly a Sikh region, from which Manu's family, whom we will be visiting, originally come.

We arrive in Amritsar in the morning. The day is already hot; and we are relieved to step off the crowded bus. After a cool drink from a street vendor we set about looking for a hotel for the night. We find ourselves walking around from one guest house to the next, all apparently with 'no rooms available.' I come to realise it is not that there are no rooms available, as such, it is because I am with Manu.

Manu is too embarrassed to tell me, but I learn quickly that it's not acceptable for a western woman to be with an Indian man of Manu's 'class' within Indian society. It is difficult and frustrating for us, but eventually we find a hotel.

After a cold shower and changing into suitable attire for our visit to the temple, we walk across town through the midday, busy, dusty streets until we find ourselves outside the marble walls. We take off our shoes, cover our heads with white cotton scarves, and we walk through the gates and into a heavenly oasis, the white marble beneath our bare feet warm from the day's sun. I watch as Manu gently kneels down, touches his forehead on the ground and sweeps the marble with his hand and up to his lips. I follow his gestures and touch my forehead down to the soft stone.

We have an afternoon visit with Manu's family, so we leave the temple and get a taxi to the other side of the city where we find the street with a large, old building made of heavy stone. There are people outside the house, who recognise Manu and gather around to bring us inside. They are speaking Hindi, and are very curious that he is with me. We walk into the house where children greet us excitedly. We walk through a hall into a centre courtyard to which other rooms are connected. It is shaded and cool inside, in contrast to the incredible heat.

There is an elderly woman sitting on a bed waiting for us in what seems to be a kind of kitchen. She is Manu's grandmother and she speaks to him in Hindi. We are given cool drinks from a large fridge. A lot of people - sons, wives and children - have now gathered in the room and all seem to live in the house.

I am invited to refresh myself and gladly take another cold shower, in a small dark back room. There is a makeshift, murky kind of loo, with a tank for water, a hose pipe and mosquitoes, but it's cool and I don't care. Children scurry outside the door trying to glimpse my white skin. I dry off, still wet with perspiration, and dress.

I am taken into one of the bedrooms with the women who

gather around me. It's difficult to communicate as they don't speak English. They want to touch me, my hair, my skin, my clothes, to gossip with me about my relationship with Manu. I am very glad not to understand them, I just smile back to cover up my unease.

Meanwhile Manu is catching up with the men in the family and I am really hoping he won't be away for much longer. After some time Manu comes back, he has brought sweet, ripe mangoes for us to eat. We say our goodbyes and leave to go back to the Temple for sunset.

Back at the temple the amber sun slips down behind the white walls. Darkness falls and warmth prevails. Manu and I walk around the lake, we sit on the marble steps our feet touching the soft waters and watch the warriors bathe. Inside the Golden Temple is filled with song and devotion. We walk through the intricately carved gold surround and sit in meditation at a golden window with the lake before us.

Outside beggars hold out their hands, hungry and in hope; horns blow, lights glare, the street bustles; hustlers with bargains galore, the sweet aromas of marsala chai shops, steaming curry pots, baking chapattis and the mingling of vibrant colours make up the night. My senses bombarded, my vision excited, India is a strange and wonderful cocktail of experiences in every way.

Emily Dawson, 31 years old, Artisan, England

Favourite Hobbies: Singing, dancing and loving

Favourite Country: Bali

Favourite Book - I'Ching

Other Publishing Experience: A life time of journals

24 LOVE AND WATER

We have flown down from Beijing to make one of a series of advertisements disguised as primetime adventure dramas, watched weekly by a hundred million people across China. We are way up in the Sichuan mountains in central China, five hours drive on mud roads from Chengdu. I am here, as co-creator of the stories and safety manager, and I am wondering where my life went wrong.

Misty mountains climb steeply on all sides, stepped with hand-cut terraces, up as far as the eye can detect. Grey and white, icy water is roaring and churning below us as we stand - film crew, director, producers and general hangers-on - on a grassy meadow, studying the severity of the river and worrying about the day. Behind us is the village of the Yi People. Da Liu, the Director, decides to shoot there first and tackle the water scenes later.

The film crew trudges along paths, past ducks crossing a stream, past r-shaped old women carrying baskets of potatoes on their backs. Here are two black piglets with pink noses, a madman lying beside them in the mud talking gibberish. Filthy, snotty kids, with their bums hanging out, tag along. Some of these people wash only three times in their lives, at birth, on their wedding day and at death.

We arrive in the courtyard of the village school and set up the shot. Our hero is a dashing young Yi man. Confident and unfazed by his film debut he is proudly wearing traditional costume: baggy gold trousers, red sequined jacket and pillbox hat. In the film he is to ask his girl to marry him by offering her a ring adorned not with a diamond, but an 'M and M' candy (our sponsor).

Our story is based on the Yi tradition of the betrothal of babies from neighbouring villages. The couples do not meet again until adulthood, when the boys go off to find their promised girls and ask them to marry on sight. In real life, these two are not betrothed to each other, but to others. The hero's promised wife lives several days walk away, higher up in the mountains. To confuse matters, the hero also has the genuine hots for this drama bride who is from his own village, and she for him. What with the film crew, the crowd of village onlookers and the chemistry of the young couple there is tension in the air.

'And Action!' shouts Da Liu in Putonghua.

The hero fixes his eyes on the bride's, takes her hand, and places the 'M and M' ring on her finger. She is dressed in a long gold and red dress with elaborate headdress and wears a necklace threaded with 'M and Ms'. ('This will be very educational for the youth of China' Da Liu had told the client during the sales pitch). The girl is thrilled with the ring and half-swoons.

Feeling he's on a roll the hero makes a lunge for a kiss on the lips. She screams, pulls away from his lips and takes off at a gallop. This is not in the script and catches us all on the hop for a moment. The hero takes off after her. Da Liu jumps to it and urges the cameraman to track the pursuit. This is amazing, more natural and dramatic than we could have dreamed of.

Of course the crowd of film crew hangers-on, including me, must run away from the bride to keep out of shot, and circle round to try to get behind the cameraman. But the bride follows us round in a big circle, laughing and trying to hold her dress out of the dirt. The hero follows, with serious intent, and the camera tracks around. Delirious with excitement, and with not a clue about what is happening, some of the villagers join the running and chasing circle.

At last the hero catches the bride and pulls her down into the dirt, still screaming with laughter, where she is pinned down and kissed long and hard. Our mission to this place is totally fake, but here are two genuine, happy, lucky people and everyone knows it, and more than a few wish they could have something like it.

Later we set up a scene where the actors are paddling furiously down the white water torrent in a rubber raft. They see a waterfall ahead and jump out to safety, leaving the raft to slide serenely over the edge of the waterfall and down into a boiling, deafening cauldron of unbelievable ferocity, caused by a huge boulder, bigger than a house, blocking the river. It is a frightening place and I am nervous for everyone.

Going over the edge of the waterfall for actors or crew would mean certain death, so in the end the scene is faked, with the actual jumping out done farther upstream with the boat tied to a rock and the actors swimming easily to safety above a pool. We come back to the falls later and let the empty raft go over into the cauldron where it is nearly lost.

The final shot is of a single cute triangle-shaped packet of 'M and M's' (the characters' emergency rations) sliding forlornly over the waterfall to its doom. It is an unusually dramatic scene, and I find that I feel deeply sorry for the packet of 'M and Ms', perhaps because the last approaches to the falls are so smooth and peaceful, betraying nothing of what is to come.

Da Liu is ecstatic.

'And CUT!' he says, and turns to me with tears welling in his eyes:

'Ah, Ah, Ooh, so beautiful today. First we have Love, now Tragedy. THIS IS ART!'

Andy Brown, 44 years old, Consultant, Hong Kong

Hobbies: Sailing, hiking, swimming

Favourite countries: Hong Kong and New Zealand

Favourite Book: Writing Home by Alan Bennett and Life of Pi by Yann Martel

Other Publishing Experience: One book - Discovery Road

25 NURSE

'Psst, Dr. Em, you want egg?'

He lurks outside Outpatients like some shady drug dealer.

'How much?' I ask eagerly.

I'm sick of mashed cassava, dried fish and rice and my chicken has yet to lay an egg.

'Fifty leones.'

'Fifty!' I gasp.

'Forty.'

'Twenty.'

'Thirty.'

'Okay.'

I hand over the money to the ten-year-old boy.

'What's your name?'

'Nurse Sankoh.'

'Nurse?'

'I was born at Serabu Hospital,' he answered, putting my money in his sandshoe. The boy is obviously a pro - he is the first child I've seen in shoes. Pleased with my little bargaining triumph, I return home to boil my egg on the kerosene stove. My mouth still coated with the delicious taste of soft-boiled egg, I crush the shell in with some rice to feed my chicken, ever hopeful that someday she will lay me eggs of my own.

Soon it becomes clear why Nurse has shoes. He totes his wares to the captive market of people waiting in the queues for Outpatients and ambushes me daily, offering eggs, peanuts and bananas.

One day I'm walking up my path when I spot a small figure bent over in the scrubland beside my house. He is obviously looking for something. Coming closer I see him clearly. It is Nurse, stealing my eggs! He sees me and runs.

'Hoy! Nurse! You…you little…' I splutter, taking up the chase, but a size 16 white woman is no match for a wiry Mende boy.

Hmmph! Thirty leones for an egg wasn't such a bargain.

My work continues: the TB and malaria, the malnutrition and the Caesarian Sections. In Sierra Leone patients usually have relatives to provide most of their basic nursing care, so why is that little girl sitting alone on a bed, propping herself forward on her fists, her lips blue, gasping for air? The pneumonia leaves her too breathless to tell me her name and there's no oxygen at Serabu Hospital. I pray she'll live long enough for the antibiotics to work.

When I check on her an hour later, there is Nurse sitting on the nameless girl's bed.

'What's that little thief doing here?' I holler at the matron, 'Coming to tout his stolen goods to...'

But I stop short. Nurse is wiping tears from his eyes with a grubby hand.

'Nurse? Do you know her?'

'Dis na Maternity,' he sniffs, 'She my sista.'

'Oh.'

Sometimes you just wish you had never opened your mouth.

'Where's Maternity's mother?' I ask gently.

'I am her mother.'

'What about her father?'

'I am her mother and her father,' states the ten-year-old boy.

'Oh.'

What else can I say? I feel Maternity's brow - her fever has subsided.

'It's okay,' I blurt out, my voice choked, 'I think she'll make it.'

Nurse and Maternity Sankoh - children of Serabu Hospital. I will buy eggs from Nurse again, even at fifty leones.

Emily Joy, 41 years old, Doctor, Scotland

Favourite Hobbies: Eating, talking, walking, writing, painting (and hopefully sports again, three small children allowing)

Favourite Country: Scotland

Favourite Book: 101 Dalmatians

Other Publishing Experience: One book - Green Oranges on Lion Mountain and currently writing 2 others

26 LE FAWLTY TOWERS FRANÇAIS?

We arrived on a scorching afternoon after a long drive. The deserted hotel, near Domme in the Dordogne, was hidden at the end of a rutted gravel path. We heard only a deafening mid-afternoon heat haze silence, buzzing flies and the tick of the cooling engine.

I knocked at reception. Loud barking preceded an unfriendly Alsatian, teeth bared, followed by a sleepy man in a vest. He repeated the word '*réservation*' as he paged through a thick book. Meanwhile a woman was screaming in the background. He closed the book, raised his eyes to heaven, and departed, leaving me with the growling Alsatian, whose glowing eyes were fixed on the most sensitive section of my anatomy, within easy reach of those bared teeth. The 'voice' appeared, snarled at me in a manner which made the dog seem friendly, threw me a key and disappeared.

We dined in the hotel. We were ignored until the ferocious Madame demanded that we moved to a table too small for our group. I refused, and she sent the waiter, whose body odour preceded him, to lay place settings. He appeared unfamiliar with this procedure, returning several times to bring missing items. We hijacked him to request menus. At each request, he stared at us with a bovine expression and disappeared, only to return for a repetition. He took the order, repeating it incorrectly several times, and brought more incorrect place settings. At first it seemed funny, as we watched him bumbling around and surmised that perhaps he'd written the script for Manuel from Fawlty Towers.

We grew hungrier and irritated, and we were told that there was a problem in the kitchen. He went to check up and a man at the next table remarked:

'Let's hope he doesn't give up his day job.'

'This is his day job,' one of my lot sadly commented.

As he became more nervous with the immense pressure of serving us, the body odour became worse and we became increasingly reluctant to summon him for status reports. Two of the seven main courses arrived and were given to the wrong people before he poured wine into the children's cool drink glasses and disappeared, his aroma hovering around the table.

He took orders for desserts before starters had been served, slopped coffee onto the table before the rest of the main courses arrived, and as his *pièce de resistance*, produced the childrens' meals, chips with melted ice-cream, before disappearing. He was replaced by an efficient girl who took over serving the whole restaurant, whilst the malevolent Madame glowered from the kitchen and the lingering smell of the waiter gradually diminished.

Breakfast was a re-run of dinner without the benefit of the wine and the efficient waitress, whom we felt had been dismissed for being much too capable. Madame helped out by casting an evil eye over the whole proceedings and breathing on the stale bread to produce toast.

When we checked out three days early she asked me pointedly why we had only dined in the hotel once. I commented that the restaurant was understaffed and could do with a professional waiter, to which she assured me that her hotel was 'world famous'. She was not amused when I suggested that maybe people came for the cabaret.

Her revenge was to try to charge me for the three extra nights. She lost, deducting not only the three nights but also the cost of dinner. That, I felt, was fair. It took her a few weeks to discover the error, and the bill which she sent has been returned, unpaid, with a signed copy of this.

Mike Preston, 50 years old, Training consultant, Spain and South Africa

Favourite Hobbies: Writing, travel, reading

Favourite Country: South Africa, Uruguay and Australia

Favourite Book: Hold My Hand I'm Dying by John Gordon Davis

Other Publishing Experience: Travel articles for magazines, internet sites, and airline in-flight publications

27 UPSIDE DOWN OVER QUEENSTOWN

Newly arrived in Queenstown, NZ, we are renting a car when I notice a biplane performing spectacular aerobatics high over the lake.

'Look at that!' I tell Annabel, 'It's a Pitts Special!'

The Rental Manager immediately gives me a brochure offering a fifteen-minute flight in the Pitts with a stunt pilot, for $NZ200. Annabel knows as well as I do that I can't resist the bait. I ask to use the phone...

'I'm Dave Monds, the pilot. Are you Mr Stevenson?' asks an apparent teenager twenty-four hours later.

'Aren't you too young to fly one of those?' I ask, nodding at the blue biplane parked on the other side of the airfield perimeter fence.

'Aren't you too old to be flying in one?' he replies without batting an eye.

Dave Monds is twenty-two. Not only does he look about sixteen, he won the New Zealand national aerobatics earlier in the year, first time out.

I listen as he tells me what we'll be doing, and what to expect. When dealing with an ex-pilot he cuts the briefing relatively short.

'You sit in front. We'll have a one-way intercom between us, so I can speak to you, but you can't speak to me. I'll ask you after each manoeuvre if you're okay. If you're happy for me to continue, raise your thumb high.'

The Pitts Special is a tiny little plane, and squeezing into the cockpit is like trying to slip my entire body into a shoe.

Once inside, Dave straps me in tight and hands me what looks like a World War II flying helmet with built-in earphones, which I duly plug in. There are no dual controls. If he passes out, I pass away.

We taxi onto the grass verge of the runway and within seconds we are off the ground climbing towards Coronet Peak. Being late winter, there are plenty of skiers.

'We'll wake them up,' says Dave and rolls the aircraft onto its back. As I hang upside down I pray the straps are secure.

Dave is in no hurry to fly right side up. We continue inverted for a good half-minute above the ski slopes and over the crest of the mountain. Blood drains into my head. I look up, and see skiers apparently floating out of the sky.

To resume normal flight after inversion the usual procedure is a gentle half-roll. Dave doesn't do gentle. He executes a sudden flick roll; one second we're upside down and the next we're not.

'You okay?' he asks. As my bloodflow reverts to normal I give him an emphatic thumbs-up.

He then does an eight-point hesitation roll, the wingtips rotating, checking and rotating again with a strange mixture of precision and violence as we roll through 360 degrees.

'You okay?' he asks.

I thrust my thumb up again. This is great.

Next he does a series of barrel rolls, and then a tight loop where I sag into my seat and feel my cheeks sink down to my shoulders. When you swing a bucket of water around, centrifugal force pushes the water hard towards the bottom of the bucket, which is why you don't lose any. Swap the bucket for an aeroplane and the water for your blood and you get an idea of the effects the G-forces are having on me. I don't quite black out, but it's close.

I focus on watching the horizon whenever it reappears over the nose, and try to anticipate each violent movement as we execute a sequence of inside flick rolls, Cuban 8s, high-speed spinning, vertical rolls and hammerhead turns.

'You okay?' Dave asks politely after each manoeuvre. I continue to punch my thumb into the air vigorously.

Then we do a bunt, which is a loop executed with your head

on the outside and your feet on the inside of the loop, rather than the other way round. The plane starts off inverted and then heads vertically up to the skies, levels off right side up, then plunges down in a steep dive. The nastiest part is that instead of pulling out of the dive normally, the pilot pushes the stick even further forward and you come out of it upside down, with the earth overhead, then climb away still inverted. This outside loop produces negative G-forces which mean all your blood is being crammed into your head. My cheeks sag again, this time flapping over my eyebrows against my forehead, and for a moment I red out.

'You okay?' asks Dave.

I am determined to get my money's worth and last the full fifteen minutes. I raise my thumb again, feigning my earlier enthusiasm.

We are flying straight and level when suddenly everything goes haywire and we are tossed about like a leaf in a storm. My head flops backwards and forwards, up and down, sideways and inside out.

'You okay?' Dave asks after the falling-leaf tumble.

I am not giving up. I lift my thumb reluctantly, as if it had a lead weight in it.

'Well, fifteen minutes are up. We're heading back to the airfield.'

I have gone green. Dave tells me later that with ex-flyers, keen to recapture their youth, the trick is to take them to the limit, but without them puking. After all, he is the one who has to clean up afterwards.

Safely on the ground again Dave opens the canopy. I pull the canvas helmet off my head. Despite the cold I am dripping wet with sweat.

'That was THE most exhilarating flight I've ever had in my life!' I exclaim as I climb out. As my feet touch the ground my knees almost buckle.

Annabel scoops me up in the rented car, and I rabbit on non-stop about how wonderful the trip has been:

'The most intense experience of my life! Even better than flying those Migs in New Mexico!'

Half an hour later, driving into Queenstown, I tell Annabel: 'You're going to have to stop. I'm going to be sick.'

Andrew Stevenson, Ageless, Male, Fulltime writer, Bermuda

Favourite Hobbies: Swimming, travelling, long-distance trekking, diving, triathlons, biking, running, kitesurfing, the list goes on

Favourite Country: Depends on the season, but New Zealand for sure, with Bhutan, Namibia, Norway, Argentina

Favourite Book: Constantly changes

Other Publishing Experience: Travels in Outback Australia as well as a number of other books

28 FUNNY MONEY

The pick-up truck careered higher into the mountains of Upper Burma. The twenty-odd passengers crammed together in the back protected each other from the swerves and judders like human packing material, swaying in one solid mass with each twist and turn.

'Ten dollars to sail down the Irrawaddy in that old rust bucket! And what really bugs me is that the locals only pay 50 kyats. That's just half a dollar. And what did we get for our extra nine dollars fifty? A roped-off bit of deck and one ramshackle deckchair each. D'you call that value for money?'

'Sure don't, hon.'

Cindy and Erroll were at it again.

Shortly afterwards we arrived at the hotel in Yaungshwe: Cindy and Erroll, an Australian, a Canadian, an Italian couple and me. Strangers that morning, we had accreted into a group during the twelve-hour journey from Pagan, loosely bound by our common status as foreigners. A man in a plum-coloured sarong checked us in.

It was late afternoon and we were in a hurry to get to the tourist office. The hotelkeeper advised us to take horsecarts.

Cindy and Erroll invited me to share theirs. Several horsecarts were stationed in front of the hotel. Cindy stepped up to the nearest one.

'Tourist office. How much?'

'One person, 20 kyats.'

'Okay, 20 kyats,' said Cindy. She turned to Erroll and me, 'Come on, you guys, he's going to take us for 20 kyats.'

'Just a minute,' I said. 'I think he wants us to pay 20 kyats each.'

'No, he doesn't.'

'Come on. Leave this to Cindy. Let's go.'

Erroll jumped into the cart.

Forty minutes later we arrived back at the hotel. Cindy sprang down and handed the driver a 20 kyat note.

'One person, 20 kyats,' said the driver.

'That's right, 20 kyats,' said Cindy.

'One person, 20 kyats.'

'We agreed the price before we left,' said Cindy. '20 kyats you said, so that's what we're paying.'

'One person, 20 kyats.' The tone had turned belligerent.

Menacing looks, like gathering storm clouds, darkened the faces of the other drivers who stood around.

'What's the problem?' The man in the sarong had stepped up.

The driver launched into a voluble explanation in Burmese. Cindy rebutted simultaneously with her own version of the agreement.

The hotelkeeper put his hand in his pocket.

'All right. I'll give him the other forty kyats myself.'

Cindy darted a look at Erroll.

'Oh, well, then,' She fumbled in her purse. 'Here you are.'

She thrust several banknotes into the hand of the driver. He counted them carefully and nodded. Cindy and Erroll put their arms round each other's waists and strode silently into the hotel.

The following morning the seven of us took a boat trip on Lake Inle.

'How many kyats did you get to the dollar in Rangoon?' the Australian asked the Canadian as we drew away from the pier.

'One hundred and ten.'

'You were ripped off, mate! I got a hundred and twenty. Where did you change?'

'Guy in the street came up to me and asked if I wanted to change any dollars. Said he'd give me a hundred and ten. Sounded okay to me.'

'You've got to shop around, mate. Get the best deal. A buck's a buck, a kyat's a kyat.'

'Yeah, guess you're right.'

We glided out over the lake, past floating gardens created from masses of accumulated weeds.

'Gee, Erroll, is that guy an acrobat or what? What do you think he's doing?'

Cindy pointed to a man poised on one leg on the tip of the stern of a 12-metre long barge. The other leg was wrapped round a pole, the end of which disappeared into the water.

'Hey, that must be one of the leg-rowers this place is famous for.'

'Wow, so that's how they do it! Boy, just look at that.'

Cindy kept her camcorder trained on the oarsman as he swept rhythmically past.

The lake had now metamorphosed into a network of canals lined with buildings on stilts.

'This is the village of Ywama,' said the boatman. He steered towards a landing and pointed to a market area:

'Here you can buy souvenirs.'

He leapt onto the jetty and extended a hand to help us off the boat.

We sauntered round the market in ones and twos. I came across the Canadian rummaging through a heap of delicately patterned hand-woven sarongs. He lifted one.

'How much?' he asked the vendor.

'Six dollars only.'

'Two.'

'Five.'

The Canadian fingered it.

'Feels kinda stiff to me. Anyway, two's my limit.'

'The price is five dollars.'

'Okay, suit yourself. No sale.'

He tossed the sarong back on the pile.

We met up with the others in a restaurant where the Italians were complaining that they had paid seven dollars for a rather fine set of opium weights.

'This place is just a tourist trap,' said Cindy, 'We couldn't get them down to a reasonable price for anything so we didn't buy anything. Whole thing's just a rip-off. Gee, I need to take a leak. Order something for me, would you, Err.'

Cindy headed out to the back of the restaurant.

We scanned the lines of circular Burmese script under which was written something approximating to the corresponding English and decided just to ask for a bit of everything. By the time Cindy returned the table was covered with bowls of noodle soup, mounds of rice, platters of curried meats and side dishes of vegetables.

She guffawed as she sat down.

'Hey, d'you know, when I got into that goddam toilet I found I didn't have any tissues in my bag. So I just used some 10-kyat notes. They're not worth anything, anyway. Just funny money.'

Hilda Reilly, 58 years old, No occupation, British living in Italy

Favourite Hobbies: Chess, crosswords, travelling, investigating religion as a phenomenon

Favourite Country: Iraq

Favourite Book: The non-fiction work of George Orwell

Other Publishing Experience: Written for several publications

29 THE SKY BURIAL

Six a.m. I awake filled with apprehension about attending the sky burial. I had resisted going. But my friend Pascal convinced me this was a unique ancient ritual at the heart of Tibetan culture and belief. Experiencing such an event was the essence of travelling.

The burial site is a stubby patch of ground on top of a rocky hill at the base of bare mountains. Five Tibetan men and a boy of about ten are seated around a fire drinking tea, talking and laughing. They wear ordinary work clothes. They smile and motion us to sit. Separated by a shallow gulley strewn with bits of clothing and hunks of hair, is the 'altar' - a large, flat rock with bowl-like depressions.

Pascal has been before. He gestures towards the mountains. Neat rows of silent birds are perched on ledges: vultures. Their colours blend with the mountains. Ravens swoop in and out of the gully, clustering nervously on the altar rock. A white square bundle, tied with a rope, sits among the ravens. The rising sun turns the drab greys of the mountains to patches of pale gold.

The sun touching the altar rock is the signal for the burial to begin. The Tibetan in charge dons a grubby white coat and a white surgical-type cap. He climbs on to the rock. Two Tibetan men and the boy join him. The other two Tibetans, relatives of the deceased, remain by the fire.

The man in white is thin and wiry with flashing black eyes and protruding tufts of hair - wild looking. He unties the bundle. A youngish woman with long black hair, naked, except for an unbuttoned faded red blouse, tumbles out.

The man drags her body to the centre of the rock, laying it face down. He begins by pulling off the woman's blouse and flinging it into the gully. From somewhere he produces a knife and with surgical precision cuts a slit down her spine. Starting from the shoulder blade, he strips the flesh down the left side of her back, using swastika-patterned cuts. (For Tibetans the swastika is the symbol of eternity.) This done, he neatly hacks off her left arm. The arm is tossed to the boy who, grunting and groaning, pounds it to a pulp.

The man in white then hacks the left side of the body, panting loudly, like someone chopping wood. The two men are thrown flesh and bones, which they pound in the bowl-like depressions. The sounds of panting and puffing combine with the squishing sound of flesh being pulverized and bones being smashed.

Tsampa, a mixture of barley flour, tea and yak butter, is added to make the mixture more palatable. It is a bad omen for anything to be left uneaten. The men pause only to sharpen their axes, or for a short cigarette break. So engrossed am I by their expertise I almost forget what they are doing.

Next the flesh on the woman's right side is sliced from the ribs. The man's white coat is splattered with blood. The rock looks like a butcher's shop, and the woman like a butchered carcass. I turn away many times, unable to watch, then turn back, unable not to watch.

The man flips over what remains of the body: a torso with no back or limbs. He chops through the chest cavity and pulls out the heart. Holding it up, he shouts to the Tibetans by the fire. They nod. He chops the heart to bits. Then he slits the stomach and removes the organs. These are cut up and put aside. The men talk and laugh, but do not break their work rhythm. Lastly the head is separated with one neat blow. The man holds up the severed head and deftly scalps it. Then, tying the long black hair into a knot, he flings it into the gully. Picking up a large flat stone, he holds it overhead, mutters a short prayer and smashes the skull, twice.

An old monk dressed in saffron robes says a prayer and prostrates himself before the rock. At this point the man in charge turns to the mountains and calls to the vultures:

'*Shoo…Tzshoo…*'

About a dozen vultures, the vanguard, leave their mountain perch and swoop on to the rock. He throws them bits of flesh. Surprisingly, they are large beautiful birds with white necks and legs and speckled tan and white bodies. Some are so close I can see their bright blue eyes.

As the boy bundles the chopped organs into a cloth, several vultures, try to steal bits of flesh. The one in charge angrily chases them off the rock with kicks and abusive shouts, as though punishing them for bad behaviour. Then, facing the mountain ledges, he raises his arms and addresses the vultures in a shrill singsong voice:

'Tria...soya...tria!'

Suddenly hundreds of vultures fill the sky, hover in a quivering cloud above our heads, and descend on the rock. As they vie for space, the ravens cling to the edges. The vultures are served with the prepared flesh, bones and tsampa. They eat greedily, slipping off the rock, in their haste to consume. The ravens join the feast cautiously, snapping up morsels the vultures accidentally drop.

After the first course the birds wait for dessert - the choice organ morsels. They devour every last bit. Finally the feast is over. The vultures take to the sky bearing the deceased with them, upwards to the heavens. An hour ago there was a body on the rock, now there is nothing. The Tibetans sit around the fire in animated discussion. There is no sign of mourning, no tears, no wailing, no prayers. I am the last one to leave.

Niema Ash, Ageless, Writer, England

Favourite Hobbies: Travelling, also love, life and the pursuit of happiness

Favourite Country: Morocco

Favourite Book: W.B. Yeats's poetry, also Catcher In The Rye

Other Publishing Experience: Touching Tibet and Travels with my Daughter aside from many short pieces, stories, articles, etc

30 CINEMA PAKISTANO

A couple of nights ago I was privileged to attend a cinema in Peshawar where they were screening the highly acclaimed *Kelapho*. A Bollywood classic, with all the hallmarks of a bad home movie, loosely based on the Michael Douglas and Glen Close film *Fatal Attraction*. With dancing. Without sex.

The cinema must have had a capacity for 400 people, and once at the height of the Raj was perhaps a theatre. Now the awnings have been painted lurid greed and the pillars vomit blue. Around us were seated an audience of seven, excluding the three of us. The atmosphere, as you can imagine, was electric. But rather than building us up to the beginning of the film we were hit with it: wham. No title sequence, no prologue, just straight into the dialogue. It surprised us - and also apparently the lighting technician, who forgot to turn out the two bare light-bulbs which served as houselights.

A few minutes into the first scene, when the light-bulbs are extinguished, it becomes clear that the narrative describes the difficult relationship between a fat, bearded man and his lovely wife, whose every appearance invokes wolf whistles from our meagre but hard-working audience. The opening scenes show how their conversations very soon turn into blazing rows, which involve him punching her in the face, or knocking her head against a wall, or throwing her around the room, or all three. Finally, after one especially violent scene, she is hospitalized.

When she leaves the hospital he throws her off a boat when he is drunk, believes she has drowned, and cries. She is washed up on a shore in a white sari (cue more wolf whistles and lip smacking noises from the magnificent seven), with her long hair conveniently shrouding her breasts from the salacious spectators.

In no time, and for no reason, she hooks up with a guy sporting a David Niven moustache. Only near the end do we discover that he is married with a child. However, he wins her over with coffee in a restaurant, where he dazzles her with his mastery of the English language:

Waiter: Good evening, sir.
Moustache-man: Good evening. Bud-bud dinding. Urdu, urdu, urdu.
Waiter: Would you like tea or coffee, sir?
Moustache-man: Hmm. Coffee. Bud-bud dinding. Urdu, urdu, urdu.
(the girl smiles; she is impressed).
Moustache-man: With sugar.
(the girl is bowled over.)

So they embark on a dance. For this our sound engineer seamlessly switches the output to all the many speakers encasing the room. The noise is reminiscent of a jet-engine taking off close by. The three of us put our heads between our knees and scream, while no one else takes any notice. They do an incredible eighties 'body-popping' routine, combined with everything from arm-flapping to star-jumps. To look cool, the hero removes his sunglasses and puts them back on again with suave frequency.

And then like that, it stops, and the two of them are talking on a sofa again. Another dance is perhaps a little more sexy. The routine is similar, though this time the man stands in the foreground of the shot, and looks aloofly at a wall. She just throws herself to the ground at his feet, hugs his legs and so on, while he declines her advances by pushing her away by the face. It doesn't really get going until after half time.

In the middle of a scene, half way through the dialogue, the lighting technician works his magic and the two light bulbs destroy the audience's dark-accustomed retinas. The reel operator then slows the film down, and a projects a slide on to the actors' faces saying: **'Intermission'**.

We sit in the oppressive heat on sloping seats for fifteen minutes drinking flat Amrat Cola, and eventually the second half begins in familiar style but in an utterly unfamiliar place.

I then realise I have been joined by two men who sit next to me holding hands. They roll up some hashish, and talk. I can only conclude that they must have seen the first half the night before.

One dance scene is set under a hose, where the heroine slides about and is pushed in the face by the hero again. It is so erotic that a man comes round with a torch to check that salwar kameezes are not jiggling furtively (his function is explained to me afterwards by a sniggering usher).

For no reason the wife and child are introduced into the plot. And to show his love for his son the hero goes to a pet shop which sells nothing but rabbits and dogs. Perhaps because the dogs are all small and bald, he buys a white, fluffy bunny rabbit for his son. As this is based on *Fatal Attraction*, the girlfriend - à la Glen Close - boils his son's prize bunny rabbit. They spare no expense and employ a real bunny rabbit for the task. Consequently, like all the dogs in the pet shop, the rabbit too becomes small and bald.

The fat man discovers his girl friend is still alive and returns to beat her again. However by this stage her psychosis has reached wrist-slitting and gun-toting proportions, so he badly under-estimates her capacity to resist. From the top of some stairs she shoots him in the shoulder. A couple of seconds later he flies backwards, and proceeds to squeeze a blood bag onto his arm. And without another round being fired he leaps back again as if he has been shot a second time, which strongly suggests a disagreement at the cutting room stage.

At the side of the gunfight the hero is watching with his wife and son. For the sake of completion the heroine shoots them too, and soon the bloody mess is brought to an equally abrupt end by the lighting technician who brings both the bulbs up, and the reel engineer who stops the film, and replaces it with a slide projection: **'The End'**. Which, thankfully, it is.

Mike Clear, 25 years old, Advertising executive, England

Favourite Hobbies: Travelling, motorbikes, reading, comedy

Favourite Country: Nicaragua

Favourite Book: In Patagonia - Bruce Chatwin

Other Publishing Experience: None as yet, fingers crossed

31 HOLY SHIT!

'We'll try anything once,' was the mantra that Dave and I chanted whilst backpacking around Thailand. After a hedonistic four weeks on the southern island of Ko Pha-Ngan, the town of Chiang Mai (a stepping stone for many an intrepid traveller delving off into the jungle) seemed quiet and uneventful.

We wandered through the streets and soon turned away from the wide open roads to find ourselves stumbling through a maze of narrow dirt tracks. The area was littered with temples and the one we stopped at had a delightful absence of tourists. We slipped off our flip flops, climbed the welcoming steps and entered, rather awe-struck, into the cool recesses of the sacred building.

A radio shattered the tranquil silence and a cluster of monks lounging, smoking and chattering obliterated any hope of achieving a calm meditative state. Bemused, we were drawn by their beckoning palms and sat amongst the maroon and orange robes whilst sipping steaming *chai* and exchanging pleasantries with our unusual hosts.

There were four of them. All young males, with shaved heads and big smiles. Our formalities however, were cut short by the monks' irrepressible interest in a poster. Unravelled, it resembled a child's chart of the alphabet where each letter has a box and a corresponding picture. In this instance however, the boxes did not show apples, balls or cats, but drugs - acid, benzedrine, cocaine and suchlike.

'You like?' came an inquiring voice which pointed to the photo of a bright green, sparkling clump of marijuana.

I smiled and shyly nodded my response.

'Me also!' was the delighted reply.

I had half expected this, but was more than a little overwhelmed by the cankerous nature of this holy place.

The next question was eagerly directed at both of us:

'You want to try this? I go get some now.' 'This' was a picture of white powder hovering near the H section.

'Heroin!' I gulped at Dave.

'We'll try anything once,' murmured my mantra and indeed, I was sorely tempted to indulge in the warped and surreal scenario. But Dave decided otherwise. He graciously declined on both our behalves and hurriedly led the way back through the heavy doors and out into the sunlight.

Thank goodness for Dave. Without his common sense, I could well be writing this from Chang Mai's equivalent of the Bangkok Hilton. Chiang Mai is the last port of call in more ways than one. In its jails there languishes a record number of travellers held on drugs charges - more than in any other part of Thailand.

I also learned, somewhat belatedly, that many of the city's monks have become heroin addicts. Strange but true. In cahoots with the local police, they set up other abusers and then get a substantial slice of their victims' bribes, fines or bail. Drug-fuelled corruption oozes out of every pore on their ordained bodies.

I'm glad I let that one go.

Laura Kyle, 26 years old, Journalist, China

Favourite Hobbies: Arts and crafts, TV/radio packages, Chinese, working with animals

Favourite Country: Too many! Nepal, Australia, Kenya, England on a summers day

Favourite Book: Grapes of Wrath by John Steinbeck

Other Publishing Experience: A story in Volunteer Tales and Various articles in magazines and newspapers

32 VINCENT LOUIS

The graffiti catches my eye immediately. I steady my torch beam on the name 'Vincent Louis' and study it. The V and the L are capitals. Both i's have been dotted. The second word is slightly smaller than the first. The name has been gouged into the rock where one tunnel meets another, plainly for all to see. Its clarity is undiminished since the day it was carved, probably some ninety years before.

Rising up from the Old Western Front in Northern France, Vimy Ridge still offers up some grim history. For it was here between 1915-17 that British, Canadian and French soldiers dug a labyrinth of tunnels 100km long. Used as a means of laying mines and infiltrating beneath the unsuspecting Germans, the Hun learned that destruction could come from below, as well as above ground. Thus all too soon both adversaries had gone subterranean to continue the slaughter. Far below ground men would listen for the sound of their enemy's picks and shovels, and set booby-traps in deadly games of cat and mouse. Occasionally they would blunder into each other's tunnels and engage in desperate hand to hand combat. Worst of all there lurked the continual possibility of tunnel collapse and entombment.

As I make my way down the rebuilt steps my mind is full of those men who had walked this way to a doubtful future. The tunnel system, closed to the public and seen by only a very few, soon begins in earnest. The roof of the tunnel at first seems reassuringly high, but I am still stooped and an occasional lapse of concentration scrapes my helmet on the uneven roof above me. As we walk out from one tunnel into what could loosely be described as a small cavern (I can almost stand upright in here), the primitive, rusted equipment of First World War miners lies about me. Pumping machines, tunnelling equipment, reels of cable and wire are heaped in a corner.

Moving down into another tunnel the roof comes lower and the walls breathe in. Now, this is the bit I don't like. Imagine a hand slowly tightening on your throat. A mild panic deep in your belly rising, meeting that invisible hand, and inhibiting your ability to breathe. Your brain asks what it is doing here. Your body tries to answer, but cannot escape as fellow team members crush in on you from both front and rear. The fact that extrication from this place is at present impossible, and that as far as I can make out nothing supports the eighty feet of rock above us, just adds to the sense of despair.

We manage to wade on a few metres more through the ankle-deep water, bent double now in a tunnel barely 4' 6' high and a similar width. A colleague, somewhat more rotund than I, fits the tunnel snugly. He blocks totally the light from the torches behind him, so the only signs of his existence are his grunts and occasional blasphemies as he attempts breathlessly to keep up.

The torches on our helmets now pick out a tunnelling T-junction. This is where we will film for, I hope, as short a time as possible. To stop a line of a dozen cavers and crew means just that: you stop. Nobody can pass anyone else. Messages passed back and forward echo to and fro within the tunnel, each merging into the next like the sounds of a hundred ghosts around us. By crouching or kneeling, compressing ourselves into the smallest possible space, we are able to pass equipment from one to another to be stowed further up the tunnel.

I am wedged now close enough to the wall to be able to trace the lettering with my finger. There is a scattering of graffiti down in the cave; names, thoughts on the enemy, comments about unpopular Sergeants and so on. The name Vincent Louis was the only one I saw, and in its loneliness down some dark, desperate tunnel it seemed to encapsulate the awfulness of the situation of those long gone Sappers and Miners.

Our filming complete, photos are taken as mementoes of us at work. Covered in mud and chalk we began to collect the equipment before starting the return journey to the living world. One look down yet another, even narrower tunnel shows a small railway track along which presumably the spoil from the tunnel face was sent back to the main shaft. A telephone wire still hangs there by its original wall clamps. Further on my torch picks out steps hewn from solid rock - by whom we shall never know, maybe even by my engraver and his fellow soldiers.

They have vanished into history. The odds were always stacked heavily against their survival. All that remains of their hellish experiences are the tunnel, the dark, a few artefacts, and a name scratched on a wall by a dim light. But it is enough for their spirits, and that one name, to continue to haunt me.

Jeremy Humphries, 42 years old, Film cameraman, England

Favourite Hobbies: Writing, painting, gardening

Favourite Country: Italy

Favourite Book: Birdsong by Sebastian Faulks

Other Publishing Experience: Selection of articles for magazines and newspapers, plans to write a novel

33 A MUSICAL MONK

The reclining seat in front of me was slowly crushing my legs, and destroying any hope I may have had of a comfortable overnight journey up through the Himalayas to McLeod Ganj. I looked at my friend Jo and laughed.

The Tibetan couple in the seats in front of us had absolutely no idea that their comfort was stopping the circulation in our legs. And having made friends with the travellers in the seats behind us, we just couldn't bring ourselves to carry on the domino effect by doing the same thing to them.

After a long journey up into the Himalayas, a journey filled with nightmares that ours would be the next bus to go tumbling down the unfenced side of the mountain, we reached our destination.

Bleary-eyed and trying to regain the feeling in our legs, we fell off the bus, fought our way through the early morning touts, and quickly retrieved our backpacks. A brief consultation with our guidebook led us up the hill in search of accommodation.

We waved to a man standing outside a yellow building, and after answering his question of 'Where are you from?' we were at once shown to our room. Tiptoeing past a lady practising yoga on the balcony, we dropped our bags, collapsed on our beds and fell asleep.

After a day looking round the markets and refusing the many beggars, we found it quite difficult to drag ourselves up the steep, rubbly hill to our room. Amused by our poor efforts and obvious unfitness, a young monk at the side of the path watched us struggling, then gestured to us to go over to him. He was writing a letter to his friends in England, and his English was not up to the task. Could we possibly help?

We followed him into his house. Well, actually, I say house but it was very small and in the West we would describe it as a shed. Inside were two beds (he house-shared with another monk), a sink and a small cooker. There was no en-suite in this little home, bathing and clothes washing took place at the river which tumbles down through the mountains.

The walls, which were plastered with photos of the Dalai Lama, displayed the dedication of the two monks to their leader, and to Buddhism.

In no time at all I was juggling tea and Tibetan bread in one hand, and a pen and postcard in the other, trying to put into words the message our new pal wanted to convey to his friends in England.

Soon getting distracted, the monk wanted to chat about other things, to practise his English. The subject of music soon arose, for which he obviously had a great enthusiasm. He quickly dug out a tape of Tibetan music and played it on his worn-down tape player. It was so pure and gentle, we were charmed and also touched that he wanted to share it with us. We silently kicked ourselves for not having brought some British music to play to him.

No problem. He had another tape which he swapped eagerly for the first one, his eyes alight. The amusement on our faces must have shown when out of the speakers came the familiar sound of Boyzone! But the real finale was his favourite European song ever: Venga Boys! Watching him innocently dance around the room to 'Boom boom boom boom, I want you in my room!' we could no longer hold back our delighted laughter!

What a wonderful contrast of cultures: a Tibetan Buddhist Monk dancing away as Venga Boys blasted from the speakers of his aged tape player, in his small home in a little village high in the Himalayas.

I love this place!

Jyoti Jackson-Baker, 25 years old, Hmmmm... Still deciding!, England

Favourite Hobbies: Photography, writing, mosaic art, snowboarding, yoga

Favourite Country: India so far

Favourite Book: Senor Viva and The Coco Lord by Louis De Bernieres, and currently reading Four Corners by Kira Salak which is brilliant

Other Publishing Experience: This is my first!

34 TICKED OFF

At 16,000 feet each lungful of Himalayan air has to be fought for. I watched the line of Sherpas ahead, bent double like old beggars under their weighty loads. I trudged on with mind switched to automatic pilot. It took total concentration simply to put one foot after another into the deep line of footprints left in the snow by the porters.

After six hours hard walking, we reached the trekking peak known as Gorap Shep at the head of the Gokyo Valley. As the sun rose I gazed upon the roof of the world. The sky was the deepest blue I'd ever seen, the light sharp and clear. The cold, crisp, morning air burned the lungs as it was sucked in. All around majestic snow-covered peaks thrust jagged spires into the heavens. To the east stood Everest, the grandest of them all, a spume of ice and snow blowing from its peak.

Half an hour at the top was enough. Fingers and toes were beginning to freeze and ice had formed in my straggly trekker's beard. The return journey was much swifter. We made it down to the bottom of the peak in a couple of hours. By mid-morning we were back at base camp - a single story wooden building which was home to a Nepalese family, and also offered simple food and dirty beds to trekkers.

Gratefully, we dumped our packs on the verandah. Cold, hungry and exhausted we went inside in search of food and warmth. I sat at a wooden table with Dan and Nancy, two fellow travellers from California. The facilities were very basic, a few rickety bunk beds covered by filthy blankets, some simple wooden furniture and a large iron stove with a chimney which ran up and out through the roof. I watched a grubby little boy of five or six tend the stove. Using flat, dried pancakes of yak dung he fed the fire. Wood was a luxury up here, used for building not for burning.

Before long a teenage girl brought us large metal bowls full of the ubiquitous *Sherpa Stew,* an insipid mush of boiled potatoes with the occasional morsel of stringy meat. We capped off the meal with a glass of *Chang,* the cloudy but surprisingly palatable local rice beer.

After the meal I chatted with Dan and Nancy about altitude sickness, blisters and diarrhoea over a few hands of cards. I was just getting ahead in an amicable game of poker when Dan let out an almighty yelp, jumped up from the wooden bench and knocked both table and cards flying.

'Jesus Christ!' he screamed grabbing his groin, 'Something's biting me!'

He hopped about, jumping from one leg to the other and clutching his family jewels in agony.

'Get it off me!' he shouted hysterically. 'Get it off!'

Nancy sprang into action:

'Get his trousers off!' she ordered.

We yanked down his cotton trousers and woollen long johns.

'It's here!' screamed Dan, pointing to a spot high in his groin, 'There's something biting me!'

We quickly spotted the cause of his distress.

'Oh my God!' said Nancy. 'It's some kind of giant tick. It's eating into your skin.'

A fat, reddish-brown insect about two centimetres long had attached itself to Dan's groin. With powerful pincer jaws it was burrowing into his flesh. The head of the tick was fast disappearing under Dan's skin.

'Don't just stand there!' shouted Dan. 'Get it out. Get the freekin' thing out!' He was fast becoming hysterical with fear and pain.

Nancy tried in vain to get hold of the tick with her fingers but it had almost disappeared under the skin.

'What we need's a flame,' I said, remembering burning leeches off my legs in Borneo with a naked flame. Someone produced a Zippo lighter.

'You'd better cover your vitals,' I advised Dan. 'This might hurt a bit.'

'I don't care,' he gasped. 'Just do it!'

I lit the Zippo and applied the long flame to Dan's groin. He screamed and the room was filled with the smell of singed hair.

Unfortunately, the flame treatment had no effect on the little burrower who was now well and truly under Dan's flesh.

'What are we going to do?' asked Nancy. 'It's almost disappeared.'

An elderly Sherpa gentleman had been quietly watching proceedings from his seat in the corner, smoking his clay pipe. He got up stiffly, came over and gestured impatiently for Nancy and me to move out of the way. He knelt down on one knee and with the long, yellowed nails of both thumbs, pressed hard into the flesh either side of the burrowing tick. Slowly, he squeezed and the end of the insect emerged. The old man carefully pinched the abdomen between finger and thumb and with sudden violence wrenched the bug from Dan's groin.

With a flourish he held up the offending insect. It still held a pea-sized piece of Dan's flesh in its pincers. The old man chuckled, squashed the bug between his fingers and threw the mess into the stove before resuming his place in the corner and relighting his pipe.

Dan was left standing there with pants round ankles pathetically clutching his groin.

'Don't move Dan,' ordered Nancy. 'I've just got to get a photo of this to show the guys back home!'

Tim Garratt, 43 years old, Sports and English teacher, England

Favourite Hobbies: Travelling, writing, reading, mountain walking, golf, buteyko, Thai cooking

Favourite Country: Thailand

Favourite Book: Touching the Void by Joe Simpson

Other Publishing Experience: Discovery Road, The Grobblepots, Billy Bones - Master of the Galaxy and numerous short travel stories

35 A FRIENDLY GAME IN KL

After eighteen sleepless hours on a plane and two hours in Kuala Lumpur, I'm about to win $42,000, and can barely believe my luck.

Earlier at the Petronas Towers, a friendly Malay approached me:

'Hey! What your name, where you from!?'

He introduced his cousins, Karen and Angel, who happened to have a cousin moving to London...

'What London like? So expensive to live there? You must be rich man. What you do?... We going home for lunch, you want to come with us? Is OK, we bring you back after...'

Smugly, I thought my natural travelling luck had kicked in, helping me sidestep the tourist sights. I was about to see how Malaysian people really lived.

'She single, I'm divorced,' Karen leaned over to say in the taxi.

Lunch, though, was for four. Uncle was sprawled on a plastic settee watching B-grade Malaysian karaoke videos. While the girls made lunch, he turned the volume down to talk at me. About his son at the beach, about his job as a croupier in Genting Hill Casino, and about a foolproof way to scam people. He explained how, in Blackjack, he would use outstretched fingers and thumbs to indicate what cards the other player has.

'If you're telling me this because you want me to... then thanks very much, I appreciate it, but it just isn't me.'

'Mr James, no trouble. I have old friend - Mr Tom Gu - he come today. He oil, gold, gay man. Rich man. He like gamble. He lose, he no mind.'

'But I have no money...'

As Uncle handed me $200, Karen and Angel cooed, almost in synch:

'Jaaames, it's fine, why not?'

Suddenly, making his entrance was a diminutive Chinese: Mr Tom Gu.

'Uncle! How you!? And who is this?'

He eyed me in a manner I can only describe as appreciative.

'Ah, Mr James from London, you very tall, very handsome!'

When Mr Tom Gu proffered his bejewelled hand, I shook it firmly. It felt like a limp piece of seaweed.

The three of them persuaded me to 'just have one little game.' With Uncle's coded signals, playing Blackjack had never been easier. It was, well, like taking money from a baby-faced, wealthy, weekend gambler. I even threw a few hands to make it look more realistic. The whole business seemed inconsequential, as if I had agreed to join in the family's ritual game of Monopoly.

However, the thing I couldn't control was the stake, and as the game went on Mr Tom Gu kept producing brick-sized blocks of notes. So, a few thousand dollars up, I tried to end the game. But Mr Tom Gu said:

'Mr James, you must give me chance to win something!'

He started to raise the stake, and when I protested that I had no more money, he let Uncle give me IOUs to keep up with his bets. I was drowning and had to get out. And then there was $42,000 on the table. With Mr Tom Gu on 19 and me on 20, the money was mine.

'Mr James, at cards you must also show money. To see my cards, you must show $21,000.'

'But IOUs were fine before - why not now?'

'To see my cards, you must show $21,000.'

His smile had changed slightly. Almost as if he tasted blood.

'Use credit card.'

'I have no money. And besides the limit is £100 a day.' The figure on my card is for guaranteeing cheques, but they didn't know that.

'I take gold too. Buy gold.'

'I said I have no money.'

Uncle took me outside the room, fuming:

'Mr James, is OK for you rich man, but for me and Karen, our share of money means a lot. We bring you our home, give lunch, is not polite not help. Please you help now.'

Karen's and Angel's pretty faces pleaded with me.

I clutched at the only solution that might take me out of there, and played along. First I showed genuine willing, and said I'd go to the bank and call home to rustle up the money. Then the cards were secreted in envelopes, signed across the seal, and a taxi took me back to central Kuala Lumpur. Karen leaned over to give me her mobile number.

'Call when you have the money, James.'

James Wallman, 30 years old, Travel journalist, England

Favourite Hobbies: Gambling with strange people in strange locations

Favourite Country: Montenegro or Thailand

Favourite Book: Under the Frog by Tibor Fischer

Other Publishing Experience: Various articles for magazines and newspapers

36 THE ESCAPE COMMITTEE

The one possible exit point on the long return journey from Mount Everest is the mountain airstrip at Lukla.

The strip is constructed on the most level surface available, which means it is perched precariously about 30 degrees off the horizontal. It is also terrifyingly short. The theory is that the incline helps slow the plane down when landing uphill, and increases the speed (and therefore the lift) on takeoff downhill. The corpses of several planes lying broken-backed at either end of the airstrip suggest strongly that the system is less than infallible. All this being said, there hasn't been a crash in the last few weeks, and we are longing for the fleshpots of Kathmandu.

Unpredictable weather conditions along the Himalaya result in an equally unpredictable flight schedule both to and from Lukla. Some people prefer to wait three weeks for a flight rather than taking the week's walk back to Jiri. Which results in a minor riot amongst the expectant passengers, who jostle for places when a plane does eventually manage to land.

When the time comes for our departure, snow on the runway means that flights may not land for some time to come. Downhearted by our involuntary incarceration Lachlan, Bob, Ian and I return to the lodge where, in the best traditions of all those old Prisoner of War movies, we raise our unit morale by at once forming the Lukla Escape Committee. There are no Red Cross parcels available, but we manage to get hold of a couple of packs of Fosters, by the ingenious method of paying for them.

At our first meeting all proposals are considered carefully, from building a glider *(Colditz Story)* to jumping the barbed wire on a motorbike *(The Great Escape)*. As it is a common feature of the entire Stalag genre, I suggest we tunnel our way out. My proposal is agreed with enthusiasm. Since Kathmandu is about 130 km. from Lukla, it will be a long tunnel, so it is imperative that we start immediately.

We decide that the dirt excavated from the tunnel shaft will have to be distributed innocuously around the airfield via holes in pockets and trouser legs, so as not to arouse suspicion (*The Wooden Horse*). A bit tricky perhaps when the ground is under a foot of snow. Or else we might shovel the dirt into Bob's sleeping bag, which is big, but on reflection maybe not that big. Or we might start our tunnel in some infrequently used building, like an abandoned lavatory (*Colditz* again). Our POW camp being only an airstrip, there is not a wide choice.

At this point we run out of lager and ideas, so a final decision is deferred till our next meeting. In the event the committee never re-convenes as the sun shines all day, the snow melts and the plane lands perfectly safely next morning.

As it turns out, as we crowd into the Departure Hut what do we see in the corner but an ill-disguised hole in the boards. It is big enough for a man to fit through, and around it there is spread a liberal quantity of dirt. Clearly someone has devoted a sleepless night to the execution of my last proposal. The other members of the Escape Committee are most impressed, and congratulate me on my apparent dedication to the cause.

We march down to the waiting plane cheerful and defiant to the last - in step, heads up and whistling the *Colonel Bogey* march from *Bridge over the River Kwai*.

Steve Kelleher, 37 years old, Australian government, but always on leave, Australia

Favourite Hobbies: Bushwalking, reading, sleeping, boomerang throwing

Favourite Country: Laos

Favourite Book: One crowded hour by Tim Bowden

Other Publishing Experience: Some in-house articles and a few paragraphs in Lonely planet newsletters

37 AN ARCTIC SWIMMING LESSON

It started off as a normal Arctic day, a very flat light and weak sun. We had floated six miles during the night and had a four and a half-mile drift east. It was rather a misty sort of day, the sun eventually just about disappeared, but because of the lack of sun the ice appears bluer, a diffused light. There were rubble pans, then some semi-frozen leads, all right to cross quickly, but the ice was soft.

After about five hours we came to more and more open water, which caused a sea mist to form because the sea is warmer than the air. Matty crossed a frozen lead; it was softish ice, but OK to cross. A sort of solid slush, a jumble of ice chunks held together by the ice floes on each side, both of which were fairly large, very much the kind of frozen lead that we had crossed countless times before without a second thought.

I was behind Denise when suddenly Matty said:

'It's moving, go, go, go.'

Black water appeared on the bank on her side, suddenly I was in, my skis were not on the ice any longer but in the Arctic. Every lump of ice I got hold of broke, but I did not feel it was me, because you are trying to save yourself you do not think of the danger, it is just survival. But swimming fully dressed and wearing skis was quite difficult!

Then I found a small floater. By now my boot and ski had come off, so I climbed on board. The floater then disintegrated under me, so another swim, then I found a bigger one, though it was only the size of a very small kitchen table and felt distinctly wobbly. Strangely enough, the sea did not feel as cold as you would have thought. By now, the lead was quite big and seemed to be getting still larger. I was still attached to my pulling sledge or pulk, which was probably a good thing.

My daughter Victoria at this stage was swimming too. She had fallen in trying to rescue me, thinking that her father would be furious if anything happened to me! She managed to find a bigger floater than mine and at one stage she suddenly asked me to throw her my camera. I thought she was being kind and rescuing my film; but not a bit, she just wanted to take a photograph!

She then got hold of my pulk rope and pulled my floater to her lump of ice. I crawled across, having removed my remaining ski, feeling rather idiotic with one boot and one thin M & S cotton sock. I was very worried about frostbite by this stage. The extraordinary thing was that I did not feel cold. I was wet up to my neck (and realised now why they had tested our swimming during the selection weekend) but because my body was so warm when I fell in, the heat had remained in my body. So, for those who think you die after one minute in the frozen Arctic, you do not!

Matty then threw a line to us, Victoria caught it, and she pulled us in. However there was an overhang on her bank, so we had to put my pulk between Victoria's floater and the bank. We stood on the pulk and got out onto dry land (even at this stage we referred to land, it is the mental conditioning: because it felt safe it was land in our minds).

Meanwhile Denise had also fallen in while trying to rescue equipment, she swam to the other bank, great high banks of ice, and Paula and Lynne pulled her out. They had the tent, put it up, and changed her clothes, but they were separated from us by an ever growing expanse of water. Denise was wonderful, Victoria said she was like a terrier rescuing the equipment; she would not give up until she was either exhausted or had recovered it all.

So on our side we had just two pulks, the cookers, a radio, but no tent. We rolled in the snow, which helped absorb some of the moisture out of our suits. Matty put my bare foot on her bare bosom, which warmed the foot, but not Matty. The foot was not white which was good news, it just looked bruised. I was just relieved that it was not my nose, and Matty a man: if it had been, it would have been nose down in the crotch... A chap's warmest place!

Luckily we had a down jacket in each sledge, so we put them on, on top of our wet clothes, as without a tent there was no way of getting dry. We shouted to the others, who had put up the tent in order to change Denise's wet clothes and prevent potential hypothermia, that we would walk north and would try to find a way round the lead to join them, and could they start walking too when they had dried Denise. I was missing a boot as it had drifted to the other side, so put a spare liner and a stuff sack on. It was very difficult to walk without skis, I kept falling over, but it did warm me up so I was only cold for a short time. We walked round a huge area of water, then found a semi-island, which we went on to look for the others. The visibility was not at all good and most of the time we could not see them. There was still no way across, so we shouted that we would keep going north.

Having turned round we retraced our footsteps only to find that the semi-island was in the process of becoming a real island. I did find it quite frightening to realise that everything around us was in a state of continuous movement. We only just got across.

Sue Riches, 58 years old, Motivational speaker & teacher, England

Favourite Hobbies: Painting, skiing, cycling, carriage driving, writing

Favourite Country: Argentina, New Zealand, France & UK

Favourite Book: Good Omens by Terry Pratchett

Other Publishing Experience: Frigid Women and numerous articles about the North Pole

38 A TRAVELLING POM

Nothing could compare with the thrill I felt at that moment. Right then, life could not be sweeter nor Bob Marley sound any better. I was free as a bird, a travelling Pom driving north on a remote highway in a rickety sky-blue VW Kombi, about one and a half days out of Perth, WA. Not a cloud in the sky nor another human being for miles, I was heading for the warmer climes farther north, and I couldn't control the urge to yell and sing at the top of my voice. For the first time in my life I was about as independent as a person can get, and loving it. Not a worry in the world. Or so I thought.

The Kombi was a hand-me-down of sorts. A friend from university and her boyfriend had driven from Sydney, via the east coast, right round the top through Darwin, and down the west coast to end up with me about an hour south of Perth. They had very kindly offered me the van on condition that I sold it for them when I left Australia and put the proceeds into their bank account. Awesome, I thought, what a great opportunity. I had wanted to explore the west coast and do my dive course on the famed Ningaloo Reef, and this was a chance not to pass up.

My destination was Exmouth, about 1200 km north of Perth, the site of an old US Navy base and a haven for deep-sea fishing and diving. I allowed two or three days of fairly leisurely driving to get there, leaving sight-seeing for the return journey with one of my sisters, who was joining me when I finished my dive course.

I stopped on the first night at a campsite just before Carnarvon, having made really good time. The first day's drive gave me the feeling that it was just me, my Kombi and the bush. Passing motorists were so rare, you flashed your lights and waved. Having got further than I'd hoped, I now decided to stop in Coral Bay for a day. Some local boys who were seriously into deep-sea fishing had said it was a top place to hang out.

Needless to say, I woke up early and got going.

After a few hours, having stopped for breakfast in Carnarvon, the passing motorists were even more scarce and the distance between fuel pumps getting longer. My next one was 50km away when the Kombi started to misfire. Despite the accelerator pedal being nailed hard to the floor, speed was still dropping. Foreboding became reality when I had to pull off the highway onto the red roadside earth, where the Kombi spluttered and died. I turned the stereo off and the silence hit me like a wall. Miles from anywhere, with a mechanical brain to match my mother's (sorry, Mum!), it wasn't looking good.

My first reaction was to pull out a fold-up chair, sunbathe and enjoy a spliff while I got my head together. After thirty minutes I realised not one car had passed, and the midday sun was in full swing. I stopped the first car that came along, which was quite soon. They gave me a lift to the next roadhouse (a 25 minute drive), where I bought a part that might have been the problem. I got a lift back to the Kombi in a station wagon occupied by three pretty, cute English girls, who were all distinctly wary of a lone man who wanted to be dropped in the middle of the outback.

My feeble attempt at repair failed, and desperation was setting in. Just as my frustration came to the boil, a pick-up pulled over and a relaxed, male Aussie voice called out:

'Need a tow, mate?'

Forty minutes later I was back at the roadhouse waving my new mate goodbye, and armed with a couple of phone numbers of 'local' mechanics. My restored exhilaration soon disappeared, as the nearest mobile mechanic was 200km away, minimum charge $300!

I entered the bar-cum-guesthouse forlornly, which was instantly spotted by the owner, a fiftyish man who'd been out here for a long time and had seen it all. I don't remember his name, and I hesitate to call him Wally, but he looked to be straight out of *Crocodile Dundee*, and that's how I'll remember him. It seemed as though he knew everything about me even before I opened my mouth.

He looked at my van and guessed at the part it needed. He

told me the Greyhound was passing through about seven next morning. He suggested he would look after the Kombi while I went and did my diving; that I should get the missing part in Exmouth, catch the coach back down, and the driver would drop me wherever I asked. Sorted, just like that.

It all happened exactly as Wally predicted, and I returned - course happily completed and morale completely restored - one night a week or so later, fixed the Kombi next morning, and it started first time. Bingo.

Then came the payback: I was to help Wally mix concrete, so he could finish some work on his front garden. For the next six hours, this is what I did. It was hard graft but worth every minute, and I was still shouting my unending gratitude out of the window as I drove off with a belly full of steak, chips and a couple of VBs.

I was heading back down south to meet my sister in Geraldton. Life could not be sweeter, nor Bob Marley sound any better. Thanks, Wally.

Steph Pomphrey, 31 years old, Freelance Media Manager, England

Favourite Hobbies: Healthy body / healthy mind, photography, travelling & discovery

Favourite Country: Mexico or France

Favourite Book: Boudicca by Manda Scott

Other Publishing Experience: Working on first novel, articles written on music, sport and hotel reviews

39 AUDIENCE WITH A SEER

On our way to meet the Nepalese astrologer Kamal Raj Bhandari, we had endured a dust-choked ride along a mountain road that appeared to be slipping before our eyes into the gorge. Stubborn truck drivers had blocked the passage of our bus, refusing to accept the concept of two-lane traffic. The bus had been halted at military checkpoints where the soldiers kept a nervous eye out for Maoist guerrillas. Kids had pestered us at the roadblocks, banging on the windows, forcing grilled maize, nuts and bananas through the windows.

Finally, in the town of Butwal, close to the southern Nepalese border with India and the birthplace of Buddha at Siddharthanagar, a cyclist appeared and led the bus along a series of bumpy lanes as the sun began its drowsy afternoon descent.

By the time we arrived at the impressive abode of the Trikaladarshi - the title means a seer of past, present and future - we were numb to the material world and ripe for some transcendental refreshment. Trikaladarshi Bhandari was happy to oblige. We found him in his garden at the back of the house, where hens clucked and a solitary cow, with its holy forehead blotched in red, nibbled at the lawn. The Trikaladarshi, in flowing red gown, stroked his wizard's beard and greeted our arrival with an enigmatic half-smile. A coterie of gurus and devotees surrounded him as he beckoned us to the platform of a shaded pavilion, the floor of which was strewn with cushions.

A single figure remained seated on the lawn, a young man tossing his long black hair away from his eyes, mumbling to himself, and puffing away on a pipe at something that smelt familiar from my college days. He reminded me of someone, but I couldn't put my finger on who it was.

My Finnish companions and I spread ourselves out on the cushions while an attendant sat beside the Trikaladarshi and interpreted his utterances. My Western cultural programming started to get the better of me, and I imagined myself as John Lennon in Rishikesh, circa 1968. The Trikaladarshi's eyes were very kind and calm and a little sad, and the word 'Gandalf' kept shunting into my train of thought. I checked to see whether I was sitting downwind of the young fellow with the pipe. No such luck.

The Trikaladarshi had acquired some fame through his predictions of the deaths of Princess Diana and the Gandhis. He wouldn't give us a name, but he implied that he had the winner of the next US presidential election up his sleeve. He boasts a letter of appreciation from the PM of Australia, where he has inaugurated a Hindu temple. In Bombay, according to the *Rising Nepal* newspaper, he has been 'promising children to innumerable childless couples'.

But his trump card is his claim to have devised a treatment for Aids, and that although none of the 256 patients in his care have been completely cured, they have experienced increased comfort and relaxation. This has been achieved, he claims, by means of herbal Ayurvedic medicine, from the Sanskrit word *Ayurveda* which means roughly 'longevity'. Ayurvedic treatments are based on three elemental principles that are reckoned to define a person's character: *Vata*, implying lightness and mobility; *Pitta*, in reference to warmth and intensity; and *Kapha*, representing cool, damp and slowness of movement.

'He can tell the secrets of your self by feeling your pulse,' said our excited interpreter, who turned out to be Sumanananda Sagar, author of *Truth Conscience - a shortcut ladder to God*, a copy of which lies open before me as I write. Sitar music seemed to flood my ears and 'gullible Beatles' were the words that filled my head as our entire party, myself included, instantly and eagerly held out our wrists. He told one of our ladies, correctly, that she had high blood pressure. He told another, wrongly, that there was something up with her stomach. If anybody had Aids in our party they kept it to themselves, and so did he. He told me 'most things are as they should be, but you have a problem with your knee and another with your digestion.'

Spot on. But a post-trek Westerner in Nepal with a cranky knee and a dodgy tummy? The odds were pretty good on getting that right, said my cynical side. A deeper voice expressed genuine inner relief at the 'most things as they should be' part.

The last of our party to have his wrist sampled was Pepe, a gentleman of mature years from Savonlinna in Finland who had been suffering mysterious and undiagnosed morning fevers for four months (and a smoker's cough for much longer). He asked the Trikaladarshi what he could do about the fevers. The astrologer simply told him that he would prescribe him a mixture to be taken in water and the fever would be gone in four days.

Before we departed we queued to buy our packets of herbal tea. Ingredients: Tulsi, Lemon Grass, Rohine, Mithaneem, Chuck Kasturi etc. I found that last 'etc' slightly worrying, but the sniffer dogs at Helsinki airport found no reason to detain me. We sipped from our little bottles of Mount Everest whisky as the bus continued its darkening journey and chuckled at the wise man and his quack remedies.

Later, when we got home, we received an email from Pepe that read as follows:

'Believe it or not, although my lungs are crap, I haven't had a significant fever since that Maharishi chap gave me that rabbit shit as medicine. It's a miracle cure!'

Later still, I realised who it was that the boy sitting smoking on the lawn reminded me of. It was myself, thirty years ago.

Tim Bird, 48 years old, Journalist and photographer, British living in Finland

Favourite Hobbies: Travelling, cycling, music of different kinds, gardening, literature, photography

Favourite Country: Thailand

Favourite Book: Too many to specify; no one single favourite

Other Publishing Experience: Books including The Hands-on Guide to Helsinki and A Baltic Odyssey - Exploring the Baltic Sea Region

40 BIRDING HEAVEN

One of the great things about chasing birds around the world is that it gives you a perfect excuse to see some of the most fascinating parts of the globe. Even better, birds can be found absolutely anywhere, from Penguins in Antarctica to Toucans on the Equator.

Trinidad is my first excursion to the Caribbean. It is a somewhat industrialized island, with an eclectic racial mix of West Indians and Asians that sets it apart from its neighbours. It is this infrastructure, and the accessibility of both the bird-rich mountains and the lowland swamps, that makes it so popular with Western birders.

The Asa Wright centre is high in the mountains, a study-centre-cum-palatial birding hotel, and once there I quickly fell into a routine designed to immerse myself in the maximum of bird species. As always in the tropics this involved rising at dawn, the first song of the forest birds providing nature's alarm call. By the time I was fortifying myself with the morning's first coffee, the tables in front of the veranda were being replenished with over-ripe fruit, the night-raiding Agoutis (think giant guinea pigs) had been driven off and the morning's birding extravaganza had begun.

In that frenzied first hour before breakfast it was hard to know where to look first. Close by, the day's first hummingbirds had warmed up enough to visit the nectar-bearing flowers. They looked like huge insects and seemingly disappeared into thin air just before you got the binoculars on them. In the fruiting trees around the main veranda mouth-watering tropical specialities like Kiskedees and Tanagers - six species in half an hour - would start to call, their notes almost as exotic as their gaudy colours.

Just below the veranda in the surrounding woodlands was a further treat: a lek of displaying White Bearded Manakins. The piebald males alight on a twig at point blank range only to speed off suddenly with a firecracker-like snap to show off in front of an alternative female on the other side of the tiny clearing, which has been maintained in a pristine state by generations of tiny but manically-displaying birds.

Down the track still further was a kind of gothic clearing in the woods, and here the stars of the show were not fantastically colourful Honeycreepers or Orioles - in fact you were lucky to see the Bearded Bellbirds at all. But high above in the mass of dense foliage a persistent, sonic clunk resonated around the grove, sounding like a Hobbit's anvil in a Tolkein book. If you could stay still long enough you just might catch a glimpse of the protagonists, positively retiring compared to their extrovert neighbours, sitting on some high bough and uttering this incredible call. Their entire bodies seem to strain every sinew to emit this extraordinary sound, which then virtually explodes from their beaks. And all this before breakfast, some five minutes from my room.

The next two weeks were very similar, although not always as comfortable. Once the day warmed up and the humidity rose, even a T-shirt and shorts felt unwelcome. I chased birds all over the island, marvelling at the flights of the impossibly-hued Scarlet Ibis at Caroni Swamp, looking like a flock of strawberry-flavoured cartoon birds as they swept gracefully in to roost over the mangroves.

I made a long and fruitless trip, most of it overnight and in driving tropical rain, to Grand Riviere in the far northwest of the island. Here, supposedly, was the home of the rare and elusive Trinidad Piping Guan, a huge lanky Turkey of a bird, but despite assurances that they could be seen here like bugs on a bumper, we spent an entire day watching the rain and saw very little else. We finally quit and instead spent a happy hour drinking rum with the locals in some ramshackle bar.

However, disappointment was very rare in this birding heaven, where you didn't so much seek out the birds as trip over them.

Russell Boyman, 46 years old, Media Director, England

Favourite Hobbies: Birdwatching, travel, football, eating out

Favourite Country: Australia

Favourite Book: Day of the Jackel by F Forsyth

Other Publishing Experience: Around the world with 1000 Birds

41 BIRDING HELL?

If Trinidad was birding heaven, then being in Finland just a few months later in mid-winter could easily have turned out to be a birding hell. Olau is a far-flung outpost in the far north of Finland, near to both the Russian border and the Arctic Circle. Its main birding interest is in the fact that its very remoteness is a guarantee of some pretty unique species, especially rare varieties of Owls and Woodpeckers - as you might perhaps expect in a country that seems to have every inch covered in conifers.

These are the parts of course that are not covered by ice and snow. This area of Scandinavia has snow for six months of the year and only a few hours daylight in the winter. As a consequence, life thereabouts is a curiously surreal experience, with all sounds muffled by the universal snowdrifts and most of the population seemingly in hibernation, waiting for the thaw and the returning daylight.

It was certainly very different to Trinidad. Here, at first there didn't seem to be any birds at all. It was unthinkable to go out birding without two layers of just about everything, and three of socks. It was difficult to walk very far in this terrain and we relied on our trusty guides - relentlessly cheerful and perfectly in tune with their odd environment - to keep our spirits up, and to tease out the local specialities we had come so far to see.

There was certainly something magical about a huddled group of freezing tourists, fortified with wheat beer and creamy salmon, standing in the pitch dark, surrounded by clouds of our own breath, through which we could see the dark cathedrals of the conifer forest. Above that rose the shimmering constellations of stars we never saw this bright at home. And then, after hours of waiting, we eventually saw far away on a distant tree top our quarry for this area: a humongous Eagle Owl. Through the telescopes it looked like a toy from Harry Potter, but its unmistakable call echoed around the forbidding arctic forest.

In this way we tracked down almost all our target species, with one important exception. The signature bird of this trip was the Great Grey Owl - few more impressive creatures are sought by any expedition. A huge flat face with piercing yet knowing yellow eyes, surrounded by a magisterial ruff of grey and black feathers, a noble plumage that covered its immense body right down to its huge talons. This was the stuff of legend.

Which is why we got up at dawn to see it, despite the thermometer reading minus 16 degrees. Actually, given that minus anything feels cold in the UK, it could have been a lot more uncomfortable. You just had to wrap up to absurd levels and keep moving.

We had already missed out once at the site for this rare bird, and hopes were not high as a meagre sun struggled to illuminate the Christmas card landscape. After an hour of searching it looked like another blown assignment, until our guide led me off on a trek to view the forest edge from a different angle. This was a good idea in theory. Unfortunately the snow had billowed here into hidden drifts some ten feet deep. Walking was extremely slow progress, as each of us in turn disappeared periodically up to our armpits in snow, and had to be helped out by the other.

But this was a worthwhile sacrifice if ever there was one. Scanning the forest edge through the telescope again, from this different angle, finally revealed our prey, half-hidden in a snowy conifer. Even though she was 400 yards away, she seemed to look directly at us, blinking those gigantic, haunting yellow eyes as if nonplussed that her morning lie-in had been interrupted.

We returned excitedly to the group, who then sped off back along the ridge from whence we came. My lasting memory of this trip to the Arctic Circle was watching that line of birders, all kitted out with enough padding to treble their real size, waddling along the ridge to the viewing point, then disappearing one after another into the snowdrifts, amidst guffaws of laughter and clouds of hot breath.

So, too Spartan by half to be another birding heaven, our trip to the edge of the Arctic did not after all turn out to be a birding hell. One of the many joys of our passion is that it is so often indulged against the backdrop of one of the world's most secret, and therefore most challenging, locations. It is a huge bonus.

Russell Boyman, 46 years old, Media Director, England

Favourite Hobbies: Birdwatching, travel, football, eating out

Favourite Country: Australia

Favourite Book: Day of the Jackel by F Forsyth

Other Publishing Experience: Around the world with 1000 Birds

42 WELCOME TO AMERICA

After nearly eleven hours in the cramped, artificially darkened atmosphere of the plane, the wide open space of the dazzlingly-lit immigration hall felt every bit as intimidating as it was no doubt intended to be. Even the large group of Hong Kong Chinese who had been speaking at high volume for the entire flight seemed to be slightly cowed.

Those distant plain white walls, the huge furniture-less expanse of carpet on which everyone stood clustered unnecessarily close together, as if it would get them to the front of the queue quicker, all led up to the line of immigration desks. Immediately behind these stood the barrier with the one-way mirrors, beyond which lay the actual United States of America.

I was still a long way from that barrier, towards the back of one of several snaking queues. Other desks stretched to left and right, unmanned and queueless. At the front of each queue there is a line on the floor which the new arrival can only cross when invited to do so by an officer. After the interview and passport stamping has taken place the officially-accepted visitor is free to step through the wall with the mirrors to discover whatever lies beyond. Somewhere out there must be my suitcase, lop-sidedly pirouetting on a carousel, easy prey for the first taker.

If 'they' wanted to keep you hanging around here they could drag it out as long as they liked. Until they let you through you were some kind of stateless refugee. We could be anywhere in the world, in any windowless brightly lit room, at any time of day or night, in the hands of any uniformed (and armed) officials.

The key to success or failure in getting through obviously lay with the green cards. We had been shown how to complete them via a video, on the plane. I had initially made the classic mistake of terming my domicile 'Britain' instead of 'U.K.' (or was it vice versa?) and since alterations were strictly forbidden, had to start again. I was now clutching my card like some kind of talisman.

The Chinese group were having real problems. The first two had reached the desk but were having some kind of communication breakdown with the officer. This went on for some time while all the others in their party attempted to edge nearer but were held at a respectful distance by another official. More green cards were issued, but it became apparent that the hopeful arrivals didn't really understand the questions on the card. (I wasn't too sure myself of what would be classed as 'moral turpitude' but decided it was probably a good idea to say 'no' to that, as well as to the 'participation in genocide' question).

Close at hand were racks holding different language versions of the card, and the first two hopefuls were eventually ejected from the desk to re-write their homework and queue up again. Another small group went hesitantly forward but it was obvious that this act could run and run. Another officer started handing out empty cards to the entire group and when it was pointed out that these were printed in Japanese he was heard to mumble wearily: 'Chinese, Japanese, what's the difference?'

I was wondering what on earth I would be asked when it was my turn. I had already composed a detailed list of my intended itinerary with dates, addresses, times, and travel arrangements. This was devised to be used by friends in case I should never be heard of again, and someone felt like investigating my disappearance. But it would also come in handy now. Rather than panicking and forgetting something vital, like my name, I could just hand over the document. I knew I might be asked about my previous visit (sixteen years earlier) and tried to remember as much as possible about the contents of the Haunted House at Disneyland, just in case it was important.

Meanwhile no one in our queue was going anywhere, and even though I had recently been seated for eleven hours, I became aware of a tremendous desire just to sit on the floor and wait. Might this be interpreted as insolence, a failure to grasp the seriousness of the situation? Could it by any stretch of the imagination be classed as moral turpitude? The other queues were dwindling and the desks were closing. I remained standing.

The Chinese had decided on a change of approach. After extended negotiations with the desk a female representative, who had presumably managed to provide acceptable answers to all questions, completed some more cards, leaving only the name boxes empty, to be used as examples by the rest of the group. During the subsequent pause for frantic scribbling the officer decided to let some others through while waiting for the Chinese to make their next sortie.

I was shuffling closer, but becoming overwhelmed by an unjustifiable panic. What would I do if the immigration officer just said 'No', and gave no further explanation? I was too old to get away with the big-eyed helpless woman act and not yet quite old enough to play the frail-but-intrepid-granny card. I was near enough now to see the stony middle-aged face of the officer and felt, with horror, a sycophantic simper beginning to slither across my own.

At this point a Chinese man, card once again completed, made another approach to the desk. There was a breathless pause. All our bloodshot, jet-lagged eyes were on the officer who, certain of his audience, studied the card briefly before throwing his hands dramatically into the air and announcing triumphantly: 'Hah! So. You're Female, are you Sir?'

Jane des Forges, 53 years old, About to start on my first gap year (after 33 years in I.T), England

Favourite Hobbies: Reading, cycling

Favourite Country: Germany

Favourite Book: Impossible to decide, but in travel writing anything by Stanley Stewart

Other Publishing Experience: Various short stories and articles

43 DROWN AND OUT

We were at Camp 2 on Everest, nearly 6,000 metres above sea level. This was the Tibetan side so there was no mistaking the meaning of the brightly coloured prayer flags buffeting about in the cold rasping wind. The messages for the peace of all beings flew from the yellow, green, red, white and blues. Everything else was muted, from the light spattering of falling snow blending into the cream and steely grey of the rocks, to the dirty turquoise of the glacial ice in its jumble of slow movement.

We were encased by tall, burnt-sienna cliffs leading up to where we had climbed along the medial moraine, flanked by towering ice ridges, sail-like on a capricious sea. Here we had followed as far as we dared the upper reaches of the East Rongbuk River, festooned with ice and swollen with glacial melt-water in full spate, for this was July. Longingly we had glimpsed the summit, guarded by steep snowfields and heavy dreams of struggle.

Our mission had been completed. A pilgrimage for peace had led us thousands of miles across stark and stunningly beautiful Tibetan lands; raw, sad and wonderful. We had constructed peace shrines from rocks on mountains long sacred, praying that our new messages would stir ancient beliefs of perfection to help bring harmony to our troubled Earth. Now here at last was the final one, meticulously built to stand against this harsh environment, blessed with holy objects and decorated with prayer flags as a simple expression of the touching of a higher state.

'Time to go down. Let's get out of here. Let's go home...'

My soul brother, GT, shouldered his heavy pack, familiar in the way of the experienced climber, and set off ahead in the direction of the fast disappearing yaks that carried our tents and cooking equipment.

'C'mon, DogSkin!' he called to the little tan mongrelly dog, who trotted off after him. Nobody knew where this new member of our team had come from. It seemed he had simply chosen to guide us (unless of course it had something to do with the lunch pancakes we'd had every day for two months!).

GT was an eminent composer and sometimes liked to travel in the mountains without talking to people. It set his mind free to find creative inspiration, and also he could revel in the tales of all the mountaineers who had lived and died in the combat for the lofty prize of Everest. And now he too had received blessings for a safe ascent from the Abbot in the Rongbuk monastery, had climbed on the thrilling slopes and was following in the footsteps of all those great men.

I lingered a little longer, spilling my heart into the wind which carved across this high sky, and reflected that one in six Everest climbers have not returned. I recalled GT, an ardent student of Tibetan Buddhism, expounding that the moment of death is all important, sometimes the whole purpose of a lifetime. As I clambered down I turned over this concept in my mind.

Glacial changes and tumbled rocks made this route hard to follow, and resulted in some wrong turnings, but after a few hours I came out on the track alongside the East Rongbuk River - to a heart-stopping sight.

There was DogSkin bounding upriver in an agitated manner. GT was on the WRONG side of the racing torrent. He was weighing up two huge rocks which reached out into midstream. They were battered by furious foam, but offered a slim chance of a successful crossing (for a big cat, maybe). GT clearly felt too tired to retrek upstream and try for a safer way. Altitude sickness had taken its toll, and now he was preparing to leap, to put life itself on the line against all the odds. It was the decision of a deeply weary man.

'No!'

My shout was lost in the roar of the icy water.

He jumped, and fell instantly into the gyrating torrent. The weight of his pack pushed him under at once, drawing him into the powerful, life-threatening vortex. There were brief glimpses amidst the threshing foam of an old brown hat and a darkened rucksack. Then there was a mouth that stole air, and a head that bobbed up and went down again…and again…and again.

'Oh God… No!'

The seconds seemed like days. I felt a strange urge to grab hold of his hat which was floating into the gentler eddies, close to the bank. And from a hat to an unexpected hauling out. He had beaten the odds, and Heaven would have to wait. DogSkin appeared beside him, tail wagging.

I wiped away my tears of fright and relief and started hurriedly searching my rucksack for dry clothes. It was then that I noticed that the sodden and dripping GT was smiling incorrigibly. Responding to my amazed expression, he explained:

'Well hey, what a BRILLIANT epitaph that would have been… DROWNED ON EVEREST!'

Tess Burrows, 55 years old, Director of 'Climb For Tibet', Climbing Instructor, speaker and author, England

Favourite Hobbies: Spiritual Healing (both at planetary and individual level), mountaineering, skiing and tennis, reading, family

Favourite Country: The whole World!

Favourite Book: Cry From The Highest Mountain of course!

Other Publishing Experience: Cry From The Highest Mountain and various magazine articles

44 OASIS OF PEACE

As the bus approached Trincomalee the vegetation thinned and the landscape became more arid. On either side of the road large swathes had been cleared of shrubs and trees as an anti-ambush measure. Now the plants were slowly growing back. Here and there a few remaining large trees stood out, many of them in the grip of the banyan fig (*Ficus benghalensis*), their trunks encaged by the roots of the parasite which was slowly strangling them.

Roadblocks appeared at regular intervals and although they were open, there was a heavy military presence. It had been a long time since I last travelled through a conflict zone. As we approached Trincomalee signs of the recent trouble were all too apparent. The scenery came complete with UN jeeps and soldiers patrolling the streets with AK-47s. Two of these stood guard by the clocktower in front of 'Trinco Rest', a cheap hostel where I had decided to stay to save a few rupees. I don't know whether they were supposed to make me feel safe.

It was still early afternoon, so I went for a walk. A unique feature of Trinco are the herds of spotted deer (*Axis axis*) which graze freely around the town. I was startled when I looked up and saw a doe and her fawn casually browsing among discarded rubbish by the roadside, not ten yards from where I stood. They took no notice of me.

I turned left at the end of the road and walked through the historic gate of Fort Frederick, built in 1679 and now a military base. Here, in the shade of some trees, there were more deer. A small herd had gathered on a patch of lawn, next to the entrance to some barracks. An armoured troop carrier stood in the courtyard behind a wooden beam reinforced with barbed wire. At the gates of the 2nd Gunjara Battalion two deer were grazing in front of the slogan emblazoned on the glaring white wall:

'When the going gets tough, the tough get going!'

I nearly took a photograph, but thought better of it. This was an army base, after all.

I walked up a small path, following the sign to a temple. Two stags were fighting. Indifferent to them, a couple of fawns browsed in the lush vegetation nearby. I felt like Eve in Paradise as they parted unhurriedly to make way for me. At the end of the path I ascended steps hewn into the rocks to a Buddhist temple which overlooked the sea. Not a soul was present. I paused for a while, feeling a little apprehensive, alone on this holy site.

Then I returned to the main road which led up to the Koneswaram temple on top of Swami Rock. Soon I was joined by crowds of pilgrims on their way to worship. Once past the garrison area, stalls selling tea, fruit and soft drinks appeared by the roadside. Buses trundled past, ferrying visitors up the hill. It was busy, but the pace was relaxed.

Signs by the side of the road invited people to pause and reflect on the wonders of nature. One of these was erected next to an impressive peepul fig (*Ficus religiosa*) growing against the backdrop of the ocean. The sea and cliffs were visible through columns of roots which cascaded down where once the host tree stood. A fruitbat was hanging from a telegraph wire overhead. Despite the crowds, I felt at peace.

Together with the pilgrims, I left my shoes in the care of a keeper by the temple entrance and we ascended the hot concrete steps barefoot. The Koneswaram Temple was once renowned all over India as 'the temple of a thousand columns'. Like all Hindu temples in Sri Lanka, it was destroyed by the Portuguese in the seventeenth century and is still in the process of being rebuilt.

The new structure houses remnants of the original shrine which were recovered from the waters below just a few years ago. It stands majestically on top of the rock, a spectacular vantage point over the Bay of Bengal. I looked down steep cliffs into the deep blue ocean where once, before the war, whales and dolphins could regularly be seen. Now I looked out in vain.

On the rocks next to me was a troop of monkeys. Most were resting, the adult macaques grooming each other while the juveniles played. After about an hour, the man from the stall where I had left my shoes came up to tell me he had to close. It would be dark soon. Reluctantly, I tore myself away.

As I walked back down the hill it occurred to be that I had just been in the vicinity of a military base, training my heavy-duty binoculars on the entrance to an international harbour and there had been no suspicion of any kind. Everyone, soldiers and pilgrims alike, seemed to be relaxed and happy now the ceasefire was holding. Many people smiled at me and shook my hand, pleased to welcome back visitors. The guards at the checkpoints waved cheerfully.

In all my travels, this was the first time I had felt relaxed in the presence of soldiers with loaded guns. This was ironic, because the guns had not been silent long.

Denni Schnapp, 39 years old, Zoologist and writer, Scotland

Favourite Hobbies: Whale-watching, travelling, writing

Favourite Country: Zanzibar

Favourite Book: J.R.R. Tolkien's The Lord of the Rings

Other Publishing Experience: One (unpublished) book: The Whales of Trincomalee

45 A CLOSE SHAVE IN SEVILLE

'Will Mr Oon Butlaire please come to the check-in desk immediately.'

It's the second time we've heard the announcement over the tannoy.

'Do you think they mean you?' I ask Owen.

'Stay here,' he replies, 'I'll go and find out.'

After a sleepless night on a bench outside Seville Airport (who'd have thought they'd close overnight?), we are longing to get home. Not booking a hotel in the middle of Holy Week seemed like a sensible idea at the time, but by now we've had enough of the traditional Spanish Easter celebrations and are dying for the English kind - chocolate eggs, fluffy bunnies, maybe a few pints down the pub...

I close my eyes and wait for Owen to get back. But when he does, he's accompanied by two policemen with dark glasses and guns. Oh, shit.

'What's wrong?' I ask him.

'Just come with me,' he replies in a grim voice, 'I'll explain later.'

I trot after them, and a policeman turns to talk to me. But instead of 'So, you like Spain?', he says:

'So, you like hash?'

My stomach drops through the floor.

'No, no, no!' is all I can say.

I haven't seen any, taken any, even smelt any during my trip. However, for some reason a sniffer dog has picked out my bag. My label had been mixed up with Owen's, but now I'm under suspicion and I have to be there while they search every inch of my luggage, and me, until they find something.

We're led into a room with no windows, and more policemen with guns. The door closes tight.

'If you have anything, just tell us,' says the first, 'We might just forget it. But if we find anything, and you haven't told us, you're not going anywhere.'

I hope my lack of sleep means I'm hallucinating, but there's my bag on the table and La Policia are going through my underwear.

They start firing questions at us in Spanish. We've just completed a language course, but we never quite got round to learning the phrases for 'drug dealer', 'cavity search' or 'life imprisonment in an overcrowded jail.' But we get the gist.

A stone drops out of my bag and straight away the police are scrabbling round on the floor to see what it is. I start to fidget as they get to the less clean section of my bag.

'So that's where you're hiding it, is it?' says the first, holding up a not-quite-Daz-white pair of knickers for inspection.

Eventually, after searching all of my bag - and some of me - they debate amongst themselves. They eventually decide I am *not* the new Carlos the Jackal, but it seems to be a close shave. We gather up our belongings and race for our plane. Once aboard we heave a huge sigh of relief and get the Bloody Marys in.

'I'm never going abroad again,' says Owen, taking off his jumper.

Thank God the police hadn't strip-searched *him*. Printed on his T-shirt was a smirking Mona Lisa smoking a huge joint. That could well have just tipped the balance, and sent us off to learn the hard way the Spanish for 'life imprisonment'.

Robyn Dwyer, 26 years old, Broadcast journalist, England

Favourite Hobbies: Learning to play the guitar and to use my new video camera

Favourite Country: Mexico

Favourite Book: Watership Down

Other Publishing Experience: None

46 BUS RIDE IN TANZANIA

Imagine a small minibus, you know the sort, one that would hold about fifteen people comfortably. Now imagine that number of people tripled; three conductors (I have still not been able to work out why); a live goat squeezed into the boot, bleating helplessly; tranquil chickens lying quietly under the seats, their legs tied together; a Masai, with his huge spear, dangerously squashed in; assortments of baskets and containers, carrying anything from bananas to the locally-made potent brew of *mbege*, packed into the aisles and racks overhead.

The pungent smell of fermenting mixes with the body odours of the slowly cooking bodies and the fumes from the ancient bus. Bob Marley blasts from the radio as the driver crunches the gears and babies start crying. On the roof the frame and cushions of a new sofa are strapped on precariously.

The bus stops to pick us up. We cram into a three millimetre square area and thank God that we are only going a short way. The bus proceeds down the mountain, swaying, lurching and braking as we avoid the pot holes, mud slides and other buses which are dodging from either side of the road to find the smoothest ride.

Further down the slope there has been no rain, and the choking dust comes drifting in through cracks in the windows and holes in the floor. Some people cover themselves but I cannot move, so dust mixes with sweat and soon I have dirty red streaks down my face.

The bus stops abruptly. Everything and everyone slides forward. We wonder what is happening; probably a flat tyre with the load we are carrying, or maybe it's a policeman coming to take his bribe. The conductors leap off, not far to go as they were hanging on outside. What is going on? Then it is clear, a family of four want a lift. No way, my body protests as I am elbowed, squeezed and squashed. I balance on one leg as the four push on. Now I am looking at someone's stomach inches from my face. More swaying and lurching. I am beginning to feel sick.

Suddenly there is a muffled sound from the back of the bus: someone wants to get off. The bus grinds to a halt. Bags are passed over heads, a small child scrambles out of the window and a voluptuous mama attempts to squeeze past. There is no time for 'excuse me' here as she ploughs her way to the door. Half the bus has to hop off to let her through, as not even the chickens could pass this way.

Then we all file back on. It is a bit like shopping - things never fit back into the trolley when you have to reload. Now I cannot even see or hear where we are. As soon as the bus stops it is swamped with vendors. I can hear the excited chatter of children and adults as they call out their wares and prices. I realise it is my stop and I clamber out, taking in the joy of fresh air and space. Maybe next time I will try the roof.

Sarah Biles, 23 years old, Starting Primary PGCE in September, England

Favourite Hobbies: Reading, travelling, walking and music (playing the piano)

Favourite Country: Tanzania

Favourite Book: Mango Elephants in the Sun by Susana Herrera

Other Publishing Experience: One short article about Tanzania for my local newspaper

47 A BEIJING PICKLE

I'm late for a meeting with General Motors. Only in Beijing would there be a bicycle traffic jam. Six lanes of cars are halted to my left. We all used to cycle on and weave through the crossing cars but today there is a man holding a rope across our bicycle lane to enforce the red light.

Two hundred bells are ding, ding, dinging and cheeky, unreasonable people, like myself, are still edging forward by scooting up onto the pavement over the broken paving stones, and rounding the white painted ornamental tree. I have to stop in the jumble of wheels and legs. This is perhaps the most exciting time of the day for these people, off to factories, offices, or universities. Some have little bundles of *baozi,* dumplings, on their bike racks. There was a scandal a month before when the meat in some of these *baozis* was found to be human.

To my left is a tricycle with a flat bed trailer. Behind the rider sits a PLA soldier trying, with a little amusement, to control a large, shifting pile of green felt army hats with shiny black peaks. A troop of soldiers march double-quick across the road, all swinging arms and obedience, on their tour of the foreign embassies. Broomsticks at their shoulders in place of rifles spoiling the impression that all is well and under control.

To the right is the little white and blue hut used by traffic policemen to keep warm and dry. Last week two English friends witnessed a policeman being hit by a truck right here on the corner of Dongjiamen Wai. They rushed into the hut and told the two guys inside, in Putonghua:

'Hey, your mate's been hit, get an ambulance.'

They came out of the hut, looked at their mate and said:

'Na, he's too far gone,' then walked inside and carried on playing cards.

My friends stopped a taxi and told the driver to take the

man to hospital. The driver looked the injured policeman up and down and said:

'No way, he'll make my seats all bloody!'

So a little while later the injured policeman died.

The lights change to green, the man drops the rope and we are off. Girlfriends and kids jump with practiced precision on to carry-racks with both legs out to one side, where they sit as though in a favourite armchair. Riders stand hard on pedals to pick up speed and gain advantage; once in the groove they start dinging and weaving.

I accelerate shamelessly through the sit-up-and-beg, one-gear Flying Pigeons on my eighteen-speed mountain bike (painted black as a disguise). I might still make it on time. I think of a shortcut round by Ritan Park and turn sharp right. As I cross the line of bikes I clip the front wheel of one with my back wheel. I hear a shriek and a dinging, thudding, scraping kind of crash behind me. I fight temptation and stop. Looking back I see a young woman on the deck under her bike, shocked and hurt. We are at an intersection, cars and bikes converging from all directions. A crowd of curious pedestrians gather and quickly we are in gridlock.

I push my bike back to the woman as a few people help her up, her knee is bleeding and black and she is just starting to cry.

'Duibuqi, Duibuqi!' Sorry, I say.

Cars are honking all around. A man in a blue Mao suit starts shouting at me. Her bike won't lift up as a heavy box on the rack is unbalancing it. As we right the bike the box drops out of its fastening ropes and hits the ground for a second time, glass breaks and liquid floods out. The honking, the dinging, the shouting man, the staring crowd, the bleeding and the crying continue. I am late for General Motors. I did this. A solution surely must be found.

For the moment I can't bear to be holding up three roads full of growing traffic, so I start to push my bike towards the curb on the corner. The shouting man grabs my bicep, shouts even louder into my face and pushes me back. He would like to wait for the police to come, (in their van with 'Wise Detective' written in English on the back door in white paint) to survey the scene, maybe take some measurements, perhaps some statements. I give the shouting man a *look*, say *'chu zhege lu kou'*, to the corner, turn and pull the woman after me; others bring her bike and the leaking box. Once at the curb I feel less responsible for the traffic jam and let them all try to figure that out for themselves.

Bowing and grimacing in sympathy for her knee, I give the woman my handkerchief to wipe the blood. A man appoints himself inspector of boxes, kneels and one by one broken pickle jars are pulled out, with the crowd helping with Oh's, head shakes and black looks. Five jars are laid beside the box. One man says:

'Zhege han gui le,' these are very expensive. I get the idea and take my wallet out. There is much nodding and I-should-think-so-tooing. *How much?* I think, and offer the lady 50 kwai (six dollars). The crowd disapproves. The shouting man grabs my bicep again. I pull out another 50 and put them in her hand. She is pretty excited. The crowd murmurs disappointment, the prospect of a return to a normal day looming like a grey cloud. The shouting man is looking for a few kwai for his own trouble, but I pull away.

With a final *'duibuqi'* to the young women, who smiles sweetly, and a *'yizhi zou',* forward, to the crowd, I mount my reckless machine and start to edge away, avoiding everyone's eyes. I go no more than five metres when the crowd lets out a huge communal (or is it a communist?) laugh, at my expense.

Andy Brown, 44 years old, Consultant, Hong Kong

Hobbies: Sailing, hiking, swimming

Favourite countries: Hong Kong and New Zealand

Favourite Book: Writing Home by Alan Bennett and Life of Pi by Yann Martel

Other Publishing Experience: One book - Discovery Road

48 THE JOYS OF CANOE CAMPING

'That was the longest four hundred metres I've ever walked,' Annabel says, shattered, as she dumps both our packs unceremoniously on the ground.

Wet with perspiration, I lean the bow of the canoe in the fork of a tree and step out from underneath it. I daren't tell her what we have to do tomorrow.

It's early evening and we still have to find the campsite, so as soon as we've recovered Annabel helps me lift the canoe again, turn it over, and shove it into the water. We load the packs and jump aboard.

Killarney Lake is one of the most beautiful in Killarney Park. Paddling along we aim for a woman lying reading a book in the warm evening light while her man hoists their backpacks, full of food, out of reach of bears.

'By the way, did you get the rope?' Annabel asks. While she did some last minute shopping in Killarney village, I'd been sent to buy rope to render our own food bearproof.

'Uh, no, the guy in the marina shop said we didn't need it; that the bears here are more afraid of us than we are of them.'

'Then how come the bears at the garbage dump weren't scared of us?'

The shopkeeper also told me there were about thirty bears laying siege to the dump on any given day. But the price of good quality mooring rope for sailing and motor boats was far too high to spend just to hoist food up a tree. I can tell by Annabel's conspicuous silence that this deliberate omission has not gone down well.

As we pass the woman on the rocks I call out:

'Ahoy, have you seen any empty campsites?'

She looks up from the book, points and replies:

'Over there, on the other side of the lake.'

I thank her and we canoe, inevitably against the breeze, towards the sun sliding slowly towards the tops of the white Cloche Mountains. We're lucky to be directed to the last empty camping site; we could have spent the whole evening searching for it.

We'd tried to book from Bermuda but the automated telephone-booking system defeated us. We'd driven up anyway, on spec, hoping for cancellations. In the Park offices we were told we could camp this evening only on Killarney Lake, and then move on to Three Narrows Lake tomorrow for another three nights if we wanted. We wanted, but looking at the Parks map I saw why Three Narrows Lake was available: it entailed a portage of over three kilometres. I prudently neglected to explain this minor detail to Annabel.

Once at the campsite I leave Annabel to lug our packs up from the canoe while I use the remaining light to assemble our new lightweight tent. I'm still struggling with it when Annabel has unpacked our rucksacks, inflated our mattresses, unzipped the sleeping bags and sorted through pots, pans, stove, fuel canisters and supply bags.

'Want some help?' she offers kindly.

'I've been camping for years…'

'You don't give that impression.'

It's getting dark and I can barely make out where the poles fit into the loops. Besides, after fifteen minutes of effort I'm losing patience.

'Sure, you put it up.'

Annabel studies the mess of material and poles.

'You've been trying to put up the fly, not the tent. Did you read the instructions?' she asks as she kneels down to undo my best efforts and start again.

I'm so busy trying to connect the stove to the gas canister, I opt for diplomatic deafness. I'm still trying long after she's successfully put up the tent. She doesn't say anything, but her silence is eloquent.

'This canister doesn't fit onto the stove,' I tell her in frustration, 'You try!'

She takes the proffered canister, studies it and the stove, and even in the fading light she can tell the two weren't made for each other.

'Didn't you check when you bought them?'

'No. If the sales assistant tells me it fits, well… it must fit.'

'But it doesn't.'

'Apparently not.'

'How can you come camping without checking…?'

I cut her off with a warning tone to my voice:

'Annabel…'

She looks round at the dark shadows of the forest of pine trees surrounding us. It *is* kind of spooky.

'I'm not happy camping here without hanging our food out of reach of bears.'

We've got bigger problems than marauding bears: starvation. The temperatures are soaring, there hasn't been a drop of rain in two months, and the forests are tinder-dry. There is a total fire ban in the province, which means absolutely no campfires. Our packaged pasta and powder have to be mixed with water and boiled, so we have to go without a cooked dinner.

It also means we'll have to paddle back to George Lake tomorrow, drive to the outfitting store, buy the appropriate canister for the stove, then retrace our route.

In the morning we set off, paddling against the now shifted prevailing wind, portaging twice, crossing three lakes. Back at the campground we get into the rented car and start the engine. The air-conditioning cools us as we nestle into the comfortable seats. Luxury.

'Let's can it,' I say, 'and find a motel.'

'We can't just leave all our stuff back there,' Annabel replies, apparently taking my suggestion seriously.

We drive to the outfitting store. I explain the Primus stove/gas cylinder situation to the guy behind the counter: they have no canisters which fit our stove, but they do have another stove for $129, plus a container of fuel. Having little choice, I accept their offer, while Annabel measures out nylon rope to foil the bears - who can be no hungrier than we are.

We drive and re-park the car, get into our canoe, then paddle and portage back to our campsite (against the now reverted breeze, naturally). Having done the route three times in less than twenty-four hours, we no longer need a map.

Andrew Stevenson, Ageless, Male, Fulltime writer, Bermuda

Favourite Hobbies: Swimming, travelling, long-distance trekking, diving, triathlons, biking, running, kitesurfing, the list goes on

Favourite Country: Depends on the season, but New Zealand for sure, with Bhutan, Namibia, Norway, Argentina

Favourite Book: Constantly changes

Other Publishing Experience: Travels in Outback Australia as well as a number of other books

49 THE EARTHENWARE PHIAL

I've always wondered how I would cope when the time finally came to say goodbye to the hair dye, and hello to the white strands of old age.

Several months into a trip through Egypt, I ended up in a better class of hotel - it had a mirror on the premises.

'Oh, my God!' I wailed 'Who is that zebra in the mirror?'

Four centimetres of pure white were protruding from my scalp before the familiar dark brown locks appeared.

Obviously it was necessary to do something immediately. I marched down to the *souk* in the village. Amongst the many stallholders, there was a woman clad in dusty black sitting on the ground with a blanket in front of her spread with 'women's business'.

Pointing to my multi-coloured locks, I tried to explain that I needed hair colourant urgently.

'Ah,' the woman nodded wisely, 'Henna.'

And she produced a tiny earthenware phial from the plethora lying in front of her.

Figuring it would be better to be a redhead than a zebra, I purchased the henna, retired to the bathroom in my hotel and gazed in the mirror that had caused the whole problem.

Earthenware phials come with no instructions, so I decided to follow the same method I had always used for hair colourant. I patiently dabbed it onto the white streaks and left it for thirty minutes.

After combing it through to the ends and waiting a few minutes more, I rinsed it out and gazed triumphantly into the mirror - to see fluorescent orange locks ending in dark brown. Now I looked like one of those chocolate-centred orange balls they have in Australia.

Sighing, I realised there was nothing else for it. Slowly reaching for the scissors, I started chopping the whole lot off. I continued until I got down to the last centimetre and then wound a scarf around my head.

Sitting on the verandah that evening, I replied to enquiries:

'Yes, I felt it was time to don the *hejab*.'

Alene Ivey, 57 years old, Traveller and semi-retired website designer, Australia

Favourite Hobbies: Travel, writing, photography, field hockey tennis, wine tasting, entertaining friends

Favourite Country: Kenya

Favourite Book: Hard-boiled Wonderland & The End of the World by Haruki Murakami

Other Publishing Experience: Articles for Backpackers Magazine and for local community newspapers

50 ROCKET FUEL

In Lao information is left to word of mouth, so it is by sheer chance that I hear it would be wise to head up to the northwest to Muang Sing near the Chinese border, where a festival is supposed to be starting.

Muang Sing is a one street town built around its market, a bustling centre of activity at around sunrise. The buying, selling and bartering is undertaken feverishly in the early hours, and the diversity and dress of the different tribal and ethnic peoples from the area make it a compelling place to visit.

Sunday morning brings a different sort of activity to the town, the start of the rocket festival, euphoniously called *Bun Bang Fa*, that heralds the arrival of the water of life to the dry rice paddies. Teams compete to build large skyrockets, some requiring up to sixteen men to carry them, and thus the rockets bring life to the town in a more immediate way.

The consumption of *Lao-lao*, the local white 'rocket fuel' begins early and continues for the two days of the festival. The fiery rice spirit can burn the back of the throat and leave you choking for air. I take a manly gulp of one proffered bottle and am left gasping.

In the morning the young women from the villages parade up and down the main street in their best embroidered silk or silver coin-adorned aprons and head-dresses. The men have mostly donned Chinese caps with shiny peaks to wear at a rakish angle.

The days are long, hot and shadeless, but full of colour and activity, and the *Lao-lao* flows. Village groups take turns to perform long, circular dances in a procession of pairs, increasingly seeming to forget the steps. Rockets are borne to the gantry on the shoulders of their teams and propped against the bamboo scaffold, where one of the more brave (or foolish) members is given the task of lighting the fuse. Some fuses sputter and die, only to be re-ignited by a gust of wind, but the first rockets are eventually fired off with a tremendous 'Whoosh!' and accompanied by showers of sparks and billowing smoke.

Results vary. Some rockets sputter impotently at the ramp, others gain a short but sharp trajectory before crashing down close to the imperturbable buffalo in the fields. Momentous explosions that shower everyone with burnt gunpowder signal an abrupt end to some efforts, but others fly gratifyingly high and far, drawing enthusiastic applause from the onlookers.

Successful flights are rewarded with the maker being borne on the shoulders of the crowd. Failure sees the unhappy soul being flung in the creek. It is a simple system of reward and punishment with much to commend it. I think it especially suitable for keeping politicians of all nationalities on their toes.

Once the rocket warfare finishes for the day at sunset, lanterns are strung out around the launch site to light the evening session of drinking and dancing. It is fortunate the festival only lasts two days. Rocket fuel may be designed to send missiles aloft, but the Lao variety eventually brings most of the population of Muang Sing crashing senseless to the ground.

Steve Kelleher, 37 years old, Australian government, but always on leave, Australia

Favourite Hobbies: Bushwalking, reading, sleeping, boomerang throwing

Favourite Country: Laos

Favourite Book: One Crowded Hour by Tim Bowden

Other Publishing Experience: Some in-house articles and a few paragraphs in Lonely Planet newsletters

51 THE RIVER GOD

His name was Potato, and he was going to lead us through eighteen foaming rapids. It was a beautiful morning in Zambia, the sun was shining, the water in the rapids was white, and I had never tried whitewater rafting before. In fact, I had never even seen a rapid like the ones I was about to encounter.

Ahead of us was the Zambezi, one of the longest rivers in Africa, and above were the Victoria Falls, one of the seven wonders of the world, and the source of the wild, foaming water in the rapids. On the previous day I had jumped from a bridge that connects Zambia to Zimbabwe over the river, with only a rubber cord tied to my feet, and somebody screaming 'One-two-three bungee!' as I plunged down towards the river and then bounced back up. The bungee jump at Victoria Falls is one of the highest in the world, and one of the most spectacular, with some amazing scenery.

And now I was heading down the Zambezi on a small raft through rapids that had names which were not chosen to reassure: The Gnashing Jaws, The Terminator and, to finish it all nicely, Oblivion.

Adorning Potato's neck was a pendant depicting Nyami-Nyami, the spirit guardian of the Zambezi, who - according to a legend told by local people - has the head of a Tiger fish on the body of a serpent. Nyami-Nyami is not a god who is easy to please. The legend says that when the Great Kariba Dam was being constructed Nyami-Nyami did not approve of the plan, and smashed the dam with a flood that killed many people.

White water rafting in the Zambezi is listed as Grade Five, meaning 'extremely difficult, long and violent rapids, steep gradients, big drops, pressure areas.' Potato went through some ground rules: how to paddle to the right, and to the left, and how to hang on to the raft if it flips over. Fairly easy, I thought, but then again I hadn't been through the Terminator yet.

Armed with life jackets and helmets our group of six hungover Scandinavians took its places on the raft, with Potato in charge. We sailed easily through The Stairway to Heaven, and we survived The Muncher.

'Paddle to the right' screamed Potato.

'To the left!' he yelled, and we laughed at other rafts that kept flipping over as we survived yet another rapid. We even found a quiet spot to swim in the river. It was all starting to feel almost too easy. We were sure we were not going to fall as our raft went nearly effortlessly through rapid number 17, The Washing Machine, and we were confident and cocky as only first-timers can be. There was only one rapid left: The Oblivion.

Either it was the river god, or maybe it was just Potato who decided that we should have a taste - literally - of the Zambezi, but no matter how hard we paddled, suddenly the raft flipped over, and we fell right into Oblivion, with Potato screaming 'Nyami-Nyami!' as if he was offering a sacrifice to this hungry god as the Zambezi took over.

We had been told by Potato many times that if the raft flips over, we should stay under it and hold on to it until we could turn it over again, but as soon as we went over I forgot everything he had said. I saw my rafting companions hold on to the raft, eyes wide open and frightened, but I had already lost my grip, and floated away until I couldn't see the raft any more.

I found myself drifting down the rapidly flowing Zambezi as muddy water filled my lungs. I tried to swim but the current was too strong, and I no longer had any idea where I was. So this was it, I thought - Oblivion, and what an apt name it was.

Then I noticed a man in a canoe coming to the rescue. I choked, desperately trying to empty my lungs of water, and I clung to the canoe as if my life depended on it. Which possibly it did. I was taken back to the raft which my agile companions had by now managed to turn over, and I heard mad laughter echo over the river - maybe it was Potato, maybe a river god - as I was pulled back on board, soaking and shaken.

Afterwards, on the riverbank, ice cold beer had never tasted so good as we laughed and joked about flipping over into Oblivion. But on the following day I went to a craft shop and, out of respect to that fierce river god, I bought a Nyami-Nyami necklace.

Satu Rommi, 30 years old, Massage therapist, Finnish living in England

Favourite Hobbies: Yoga, travelling, cycling

Favourite Country: India

Favourite Book: The Satanic Verses by Salman Rushdie

Other Publishing Experience: Various travel articles

52 ANYONE FOR SHUFFLEBOARD?

We wondered which four of the mostly elderly and infirm passengers waiting at the terminal would be joining us two fit fifty-somethings for the duration of our cruise.

We arrived at our allotted dining table and our companions did not disappoint us. The ice was broken immediately with introductions all round. One couple had not cruised before so, in the tradition of such seasoned travellers as we, they were regaled with advice on etiquette, trips to take/not to take, etc. Well, it was our third cruise, and the second for the other couple.

I was always given to understand that one either loved cruises or hated them, with no in-between. Personally, I am ambivalent. I like lazing on a different beach practically every other day, but am not one for shuffleboard, deck quoits and bingo, not to mention afternoon tea heralded by a bell.

It was a pleasure to have the very experienced and charming Chief Engineer join us for dinner on each formal occasion. His hospitality drastically reduced our bar bill, though not as drastically as on our first cruise, when we got no bill at all - apparently they were all blown overboard.

Having crossed the Bay of Biscay - three queasy days for the majority of passengers - we arrived in Madeira. Visits followed to four of the Canary Islands, where, sadly, we lost the Ship's Doctor due to a fatal heart attack. We looked forward to stopping at Gibraltar - shop till we drop, whisky and presents galore!

The ship slowed down and an announcement confirmed that one of the engines was experiencing a problem. The good news was that we would miss Ceuta and arrive in Gibraltar later than planned, but stay longer. Shopping was back on the agenda. Then we heard we would miss Gibraltar and continue, slowly, to our next destination of Vigo. No problem! I had found my niche on the top deck, and was free to do absolutely nothing but chill out and sunbathe.

The reaction to these developments was mostly good-humoured. We did wonder whether our postcards had yet been forwarded from the ship, feeling we might retrieve and amend them to say: 'Wish you were here - instead of us!'

Eventually it became apparent that the ship was irreparable. We missed Vigo and sailed to Lisbon, which was not on the itinerary and from whence a flight home had been arranged. Fine by me - more sunbathing, no long sail to Southampton that would have become colder each day (in March).

On terra firma once more, our misadventures were met with mirth. We hastened to reassure friends that the setbacks were unavoidable, we were well informed, in no immediate danger and it was not a disaster. In truth however, we had all been a bit thoughtful when we were told the crew was checking oars and provisions in the lifeboats.

But we have pleasant memories of new friends and places previously unvisited - and the extra sea-time provided an unexpected bonus: I am now an accomplished shuffleboarder!

An explanatory letter followed, with an apology for curtailing our cruise by two days. It was accompanied by a cheque, which certainly enables a future booking - but perhaps on a sister ship.

Angela Moss, 59, Local Government officer, England

Favourite Hobbies: Golf, bridge, swimming, enjoying my family

Favourite Country: England

Favourite Book: Captain Corelli's Mandolin

Other Publishing Experience: None

53 IMAGES OF CAIRO

Reflections fascinate me, especially multiple images fragmented and juxtaposed at angles on window panes. The windows on the rounded 'corner' of this particular building were set facing different directions on a curved wall. I took a picture of the complete windows from a distance as I approached. As I got closer I lifted my camera to capture more details of the framed skyline.

A passer-by frantically waved his arms at me:

'No photo, no photo.'

I raised my eyebrows, questioning, shrugged my shoulders, and ostensibly put my camera away.

Further down the street I crossed the road. In the shop windows were more reflections of the windows I had first seen. I took more photos, changed the film, and took a few more shots. I wandered into a new shopping mall. Hungry, I bought a Mars bar.

'These policemen want your film, or you must go with them,' said the young man as he gave me my change. I turned round to find four young men standing behind me, talking into their mobile phones. They had no uniforms - and no English.

With the shop assistant's help they explained that it is forbidden to photograph Government buildings in Egypt. I did know that. What I did not know was that this new building belonged to the Government. Actually the building work was unfinished, still unoccupied. I suggested that if they had a sign up, in English, saying it was a government building I would not have taken a photograph. As there was no identification of the building, how was I supposed to know what it was? I discovered later that even the local people didn't know what the building was.

They demanded the film from my camera. Then they understood my mime that it was the film in my bag that had the forbidden photo on it, not the one in my camera.

I asked to make a phone call, I was due to meet an Egyptian friend. The assistant handed me a telephone, and I told my friend why I would be delayed. She spoke to the officers, and then assured me that it was OK to go with them. They explained to her that if I went with them they would develop the film and give me all the photos except the one of that building. As it was a slide film I needed to be sure that they understood, so that they did not ruin the entire film by processing it incorrectly.

I was taken through a small gap in the hoardings, there was nothing to suggest that this was a police station, as they had said. I was asked to sit down, and left waiting in a comfortable chair in a small room. They took my passport away, and I was left on my own.

Eventually a very senior ranking official came and spoke to me in English. I explained about the slide film. He was very courteous, assured me they would process the film and took down my address in Cairo so that they could send the rest of the slides to me. He wanted to know why I had chosen to photograph this particular building. He listened politely while I explained that I was interested in the patterns and reflections on the glass, not in the building itself, and that I use these images to develop abstract designs for woven wall-hangings. He made small talk, and apologised for keeping me waiting and causing me any inconvenience. His manner was impeccable.

Then he went off to attend to his other duties, leaving his junior officer to make a note of all my details. I pointed out that all these were on my passport, which they had taken away. Then I was left alone again for ages, before my passport was finally returned and I was led back out to the street.

I spent several more days in Cairo before going back home to the UK - without the missing film.

A couple of months later I went off to Nepal for a few weeks. After I was home again I wondered if it was worth trying to contact the authorities to ask for my film, but thought they would only use their inefficient postal system as an excuse that it was lost - my postcard to my husband had only just arrived.

A few weeks later a small package arrived with a London

postmark. It contained two boxes and a letter from the Egyptian embassy, apologising for any misunderstanding. One box contained 35 slides, and the other their gift of a silver bracelet with delicately carved images of ancient Egyptian Queens.

Impressive, I thought.

Susan Garrett Wright, 59 years old, Contemporary basketmaker, England

Favourite Hobbies: Listening to classical and world music, visual arts and traditional ethnic textiles

Favourite Country: Tibet

Favourite Book: Full Tilt on a Bicycle by Dervla Murphy

Other Publishing Experience: None

54 CHINESE WATER TORTURE

To celebrate the purchase of our condo in Jomtien my daughter, two young grandsons and I walked up the road to have a meal at a German restaurant. We returned to the condo at about 10.30pm.

When we arrived in our room we realised there was water dripping into the bath from the ceiling tiles. The drip line started to spread so I went and got the security guard, who didn't speak English, and made him follow me to the room. I showed him the drips, he shrugged his shoulders and left. More drips, another security guard, same result.

I then went up to the next floor, the fourth, to the room directly above us. Water was pouring from under the door, and the hallway was flooded. So back to the security guard, who by this time had gone to the next building. Found another one, grabbed him by the sleeve and made him follow me, back to the fourth floor. He turned off the mains water to the room, shrugged his shoulders and left. I located another tenant wandering around with a tap fitting, who spoke English and took him to the security guard and asked him to make three points to the security guard:

(a) As tap, lights and air-conditioning were all going in the fourth floor room, was the tenant alright?

(b) My room urgently needed attention, as the water was now dripping out of the bathroom, foyer and bedroom ceilings into our room.

(c) Specifically, could we have more towels urgently, to mop up the spreading puddles in our room, as our own towels were now sodden.

The security guard's answers were (a) shrug (b) shrug (c) no.

Next question?

Did they have a phone or mobile so that I could ring David, the real estate agent (no) and (no) but there was a phone box downstairs that I could use with a card phone.

Next question?

OK, where can I buy a card? Answer: from the office. So I said I would go to the office to purchase a phone card, only to be informed that the office didn't open till the morning. In the end they decided that if I walked back up the road to the 7 Eleven I could get a local phone card and ring David. Time now 11.30pm. Fortunately one of the young security guards had one, which he lent me so I gave him 100baht. I rang David, who brought some towels, asked for reports, and said the building management office would fix it. The maintenance man drilled holes in the ceiling to facilitate the water drainage. So we went to sleep with the (new) bed pulled out, towels on the floor and water dripping in both the bath and the bucket at the head of the bed.

The tenants upstairs had bought two apartments side by side, lined them with very expensive marble and covered up the overflow drains in the bathroom floor. Their whole apartment was flooded, water running out of the door into the corridor and out of the other side of their condo off the balcony. They had left the tap running and had gone up the road to have dinner.

Melissa wanted to ring home, at what would have been 6.30am (NZ) but I told her no one in New Zealand could stop our ceiling dripping and we only had a domestic phone card, not an international card.

Anyway it is all going to be fixed. Apparently the maintenance men do a good job, the building is concrete, and they just wait for it all to dry, re-plaster and re-paint.

Never mind. No problem.

Jenny Williams, 50 years old, Matriarch, New Zealand

Favourite Hobbies: Traveling to Thailand, pottery (as in ceramics) and drinking tea

Favourite Country: Mad, crazy, chaotic, wonderful Thailand

Favourite Book: Now We Are Six by A.A. Milne

Other Publishing Experience: None

55 THE CURSE OF APACHE

When staying in the colonial town of San Cristóbal de las Casas, in the cool highlands of the Mexican state of Chiapas, it is customary to visit San Juan Chamula, a nearby Tzotzil Maya village renowned for remarkable religious rituals. It is also customary to make the ten-kilometre journey on horseback. What better way, I asked myself, to see the countryside? (I later realised the answer to that question is 'from the car').

Enrique, a young tour guide, effervesced with enthusiasm for riding trips to San Juan Chamula. He seemed calm and confident. This, I assumed, all stemmed from a long-held passion for horses. He was probably running a family business built up over generations.

Not so. When the Spanish invaded Mexico in the early 16th century, the horse gave them a significant military advantage. It improved physical dominance in battle and played on the superstitious nature of local tribes, who had never seen horses before. It seemed that this unfamiliarity with the equine form had been passed down over almost 500 years, undiluted, to Enrique.

I paid the not-inconsiderable fee and was driven, with a few other tourists, to some stables on the outskirts of San Cristóbal. (I say stables, because I have failed to find a word for a loosely fenced patch of dust, with a decaying wooden shack and an equestrian function.)

The shack seemed an unlikely storehouse for the riding equipment. I was in the middle of wondering if it would contain a riding hat big enough for me, when Enrique, waving in the shack's general direction, clarified matters:

'Anyone need the toilet?'

Then he jabbed a finger at me and adopted a strongman pose:

'*Fuertote!*'

His procedure for allocating horses to riders was based not on ability or experience, but solely on the size of the rider. Under this system, all professional jockeys would have received a smaller horse than me. My heart rate ticked up a notch or two.

'Apache,' barked Enrique. One of his helpers, who seemed to be cowering away from the animal, led over a large stallion.

After mounting - on the fifth attempt and with assistance - I took stock: no hats, no safety lecture, no run-down on equestrian basics, no stables and an assessment system that rated me above Lester Piggott. I felt weak. (I had had a similar feeling in a helicopter on Rio de Janeiro's Sugarloaf mountain a second after it had taken off: it occurred to me that I knew nothing about the helicopter company's safety record and should at least have made a polite enquiry about the pilot's nervous tick.)

Thankfully, I was not a complete novice. I had once been led slowly around a Dorset field on Sunshine - technically a pony - when I was eight, and was no stranger to a donkey ride.

At the first sign of open countryside, Apache thundered off.

I had come directly to San Cristóbal from Oaxaca state, where I had spent three weeks on the beach at a place called Zipolite. The stay had involved occasional trips to the sea and the bar, but the vast bulk of my time had been spent in a hammock. I was extremely familiar with gentle lateral movement. With its violent vertical motion and brutal forward thrust, this was different. There was certainly nowhere to balance a drink.

Words such as 'flailing' and 'rag doll' raced through my mind, colliding with visions of cordoned-off areas and news reporters sighing into TV cameras about this 'hopelessly amateur outfit'. As I watched rocks fly past at 40 kilometres an hour, I wondered how the horse's smooth hooves gripped such slippery ground. My view of the countryside was unforgettable, but I was too close to it and it was moving too fast to get much of a sense of the landscape.

Every now and then a change in terrain would force

Apache to slow down. The others would begin to catch up and, over my shoulder, I would hear Enrique yelling at me to pull the reins - as useful as being instructed to control a fire by throwing water on it. Needless to say, this had occurred to me, but Apache, wise to my inexperience, had the bit between his teeth.

Despite the soreness, my first impressions of the village were positive, my spirits buoyed by having cheated death.

The villagers fuse Mayan beliefs with Christian iconography and, although there was nothing extraordinary about the village, which consisted of a handful of basic buildings, the church's interior was spectacular. A scene from a Hieronymous Bosch painting, it swarmed with worshippers, some seated, some lying prostrate under a curtain of incense, making offerings (eggs, mainly) to gods represented by Christian saints.

Cameras were forbidden. The worshippers believe that having their photograph taken equates to theft of the soul and are liable to seek revenge. Someone said two tourists had been stoned to death the previous year for the same offence. Perhaps I had underestimated Enrique's planning skills - perhaps today's entertainment was a cleverly themed religious experience, with the horse-ride representing my descent to hell, and the church, with its manic eeriness and the penchant of its inhabitants for murdering visitors, as hell itself.

My hands were lacerated and the first signs of the walking and seating difficulties that would plague me for the next week had begun to emerge. The ubiquitous wild dogs on the road to San Cristóbal made walking back even less attractive than riding, so I asked Enrique to swap horses with me for the return. After his initial refusal, our group, including his own helpers, rounded on him. The words *'responsabilidad'* and 'instructor' wafted in and out of the lively discussion.

Eventually, he gave in. Watching him vanish into the distance, being tossed helplessly around, I mounted Enrique's docile horse, Nancy. The gentle swaying reminded me of Zipolite. Since then I have tended to favour hammock-style activities when travelling. And I heard that shortly after his ride on Apache Enrique quit the horse game for good.

Tom Nicholls, 34 years old, Journalist, England

Favourite Hobbies: Writing (film scripts and comedy), performing comedy, cooking, reading

Favourite Country: Spain

Favourite Book: Crime and Punishment

Other Publishing Experience: Numerous business journalism articles

56 PICTURES COME TO LIFE

As a musician I was greatly interested in the music I would be hearing in Java. For months before departure I read all the books I could find about the Gamelan Orchestra. I loved the pictures of the intricately carved wooden cradles that held the metal keys of the glockenspiel-type instruments. The gleaming bronze domes of the small gongs and the huge, ornate support structure for the great big gongs absolutely fascinated me. What would they actually sound like? Recordings were never the same, and I couldn't wait to hear for myself.

My expensive 'Insight Guide' book had on the front cover a photograph of one of the Palace Guards from Central Java. He was an elderly man who stood ramrod straight in his traditionally batik-patterned sarong, perhaps because of the sword he had stuck in the sash, down his back. On his head he wore a sort of turban of matching material, and the profile of his face was lined and proud, with a tiny inscrutable smile. He looked so dignified. I wondered whether the Palace still had these guards.

My train pulled in at Yogyakarta station, Central Java, and after settling in at my little hotel I found a becak to take me to the Palace. The becak was a bicycle pedicab that projects the passenger suicidally into the hurtling traffic before the driver. It's amazing that there aren't more accidents, but I'd got used to shutting my eyes tightly at particularly hairy moments and, by thus avoiding seeing the narrow misses, my nerves remained reasonably intact.

The Kraton (Palace) belongs to the Sultan of Yogya and his family. Foreign officials and Heads of State are entertained within its white marbled buildings, many of which have no sides, just a roof and brightly decorated pillars. I'd walked slowly through the throng of hawkers just outside, who sold everything from vegetables to postcards, tooled leather lampshades and souvenir wavy swords (Kris) in fancy brass scabbards.

Once inside the Palace walls there was instant peace and tranquillity. There were very few people about, but suddenly I came face to face with the man from my guide book front cover. I couldn't believe it! He wasn't exactly the same person, but his age, his elegant and proud demeanor, his clothing and polite gentility had stepped off that page and into my life.

'Speak English?' he asked, in a gentle, halting voice. I nodded, open-mouthed.

'Then I be your guide.'

And I spent the next couple of hours being slowly and quietly led from one fascinating area to another by this old retainer, whose entire family worked for the Royals in one way or another. His voice never rose above a quiet murmur, and he exuded respect for his employers. There were other Palace Guards around, tidying up, re-painting parts of the patterned pillars, planting new tubs, all elderly and obviously very loyal.

Then there it was. I stopped in my tracks as I suddenly heard the unmistakable sounds of Gamelan Gongs.

'Where are they playing?' I asked my guide, who gestured forward with a gentle wave of his arm.

'The Gamelan orchestra they practice for the Ramayana ballet,' he said. This was getting better. And when was the ballet? That very evening!

I quickened my pace as the gongs grew louder and round the next corner, sitting on the marble floor of a pavilion, were my imagined musicians. There were fifteen of them, by the look of them all aged well over sixty-five, wearing matching sarongs and turbans of the Kraton's own batik pattern. They sat on red velvet cushions, each playing his own variety of Gamelan instrument in hypnotically repeating cycles. The small glock-type instruments sounded like tinkling water against the mellowness of the tea-pot sized gongs. The quiet, nasal two-stringed fiddle played strange, haunting melodies and the bamboo flute sounded like a husky bird twittering. And every so often, the physically bone-jarring, ear-hammering strike of a giant gong would reverberate for several moments as the magical sounds continued.

The players' faces showed no emotion, their concentration was intense and absolute. Occasionally they'd glance down at a piece of paper which presumably had the tune-patterns on it, but mostly they seemed entranced by their own sounds. I was absolutely fascinated. The pictures had jumped off the pages of my books and were in front of me as vibrant life-forms. There was no audience, I was their sole, privileged spectator.

I stood transfixed for about fifteen minutes, uncontrollable tears on my cheeks, and was at the height of my reverie when suddenly one of the musicians looked at his watch, gave an unintelligible shout and as a single unit they all downed tools, pulled out their clove cigarettes and burst into loud chatter, laughter and beaming, toothless grins. It was TEA BREAK.

Snapping back to reality, I complimented them enthusiastically on their music in a mixture of pidgin English, nods, thumbs-ups and handshakes. They were all very friendly and happily posed for photographs.

That evening I made my way in the dark back to the Kraton, and this time I was seated in an outdoor auditorium that sloped gently down to a polished stage. My Gamelan friends were lined along the back of the stage with their instruments ready. There was a low murmuring from the audience of mixed tourists and Javanese as they pointed things out to each other, then the magic began.

The Ramayana Ballet is to Indonesia what the Royal Ballet Company of Covent Garden is to Britain. The highly trained dancers told us stories from the epic poem using liquid, stylised movements in perfect synchronisation. Their costumes and head-dresses were stunning, liberally threaded with gold and colours of peacock intensity. The music and the dancing perfectly complemented one another, now slow and dreamy, now dramatic and exciting.

I felt transported to Wonderland, and was so sorry when it ended. It closed a magic chapter of my unforgettable journey through Indonesia.

Marcelle Douglas, 52 years old, School music teacher, England

Favourite Hobbies: Photography, music activities, learning to draw & sketch, travelling to new places

Favourite Country: Indonesia

Favourite Book: Running a Hotel on the Roof of the World - Five Years in Tibet by Alec Le Sueur

Other Publishing Experience: None, but keep amusing diaries of travels

57 A PAINFUL OUTING

'See you again', smiled the sign breezily as we sped out of town.

'I doubt it,' I thought, as I sat on the back of a motorbike, feeling very frightened, clinging to the waist of a man I'd met in the street five minutes ago. I wanted to get off but I was supposed to be having fun.

I was on a 'day out' with the 'Easy Riders,' a group of middle-aged bikers who act as informal tour guides taking travellers, on the back of their 250cc Hondas, out into the lush-green-and-red-earth coffee-growing hills of Central Vietnam. Touted throughout the backpacking brotherhood as *the* people to show you the 'real' Vietnam, I'd been bugging my fellow rucksack bearers to accompany me on one of their trips since our first banana pancakes on the infamous Khao San Road, at the start of our tour round Southeast Asia.

'We've got to go on a trip with them,' I had said.

'It'll be brilliant,' I had said.

'I love motorbikes,' I had said.

'We *have* to get off the backpacker trail,' I had said.

'This isn't *real* travelling,' I whined on, hoping they would feel pathetic and pedestrian in the face of my lust for adventure. What I failed to remember was I also *love* being in control. I remembered later. Back then I was only concerned with tracking down the Easy boys.

'You don't need to find them, they'll find you,' everyone had said to us.

They did, late one morning, as we strolled through their hometown of Dalat.

'Hello,' said a man whom we came to know as Thong, 'I'm an Easy Rider.'

And out came his books, full of testimonials written by

previous pillion passengers. A quick read-through made it clear, if we jumped on the back of Thong's bike we'd join a global association of happy customers for whom a day out with the Easies had been the highlight of their stay in Vietnam and, for some, their lives.

Greg and Carol from Portsmouth couldn't recommend it enough. According to them there was no better way to see Vietnam. Not only had they shared meals with those elusive tourist attractions, the-ethnic-minority-tribespeople-who-haven't-seen-many-westerners-before, they had also swum in pristine waterfalls, chatted with farmers and played with poor Vietnamese children.

Katie and Ben from Brisbane had found themselves having such a riot they'd been unwilling to separate themselves from the saddle, and signed up for a ten-day tour around Southern Vietnam. They had spent their evenings listening to war stories, watered down with strong spirits drunk from clay pots around the campfire. And all the entries confirmed the hype; Easy Riders were *the* people to show you the 'Real Vietnam'. We signed up immediately.

Thong was happy, but explained there had been a run on Easy Riders that morning so he would have to round up some substitutes. He came back with a stubbly metal-toothed freedom fighter who looked as though he might have had a busy night blowing up oil pipes in Chechnya and, what appeared to be a young teenager who had borrowed his Dad's bike for the day. I decided Thong was mine and left my partners with the two wannabes.

The day started well. I put on my sunglasses and held on to the back of the bike with just one hand. We were I thought cool, young, independent travellers, out on the road, grabbing all the adventures life threw at us. We wound in an out of the traffic and visited Crazy House, a half-finished hotel designed by the bohemian offspring of a previous Vietnamese president, with rooms designed on animal themes like 'Pheasant room' - one for the British apparently - and 'Bear Room' for the Russians.

Next stop was Chicken Village, an ethnic minority village, playing host to a huge concrete chicken. It sounded good but before we got there things started to go wrong. As the houses became sparser, and the road stretched out into the valley ahead, Thong's right hand - also the only part of his upper body in contact with the bike - twisted around the handle-bar and opened up the throttle.

The tarmac beneath my bare toes was transformed into a menacing blur, and I was transformed into a mass of pure panic.

'Fuck,' I cried but my little yelp of anguish was snatched silently into our slipstream.

'Fucking hell, I fucking hate this,' I screamed louder, digging my hands hard into Thong's ribs as the nearest things I could find to brakes.

'It's OK,' he said, 'I am a good driver.'

I'm sure he was. And, if I could have taken my petrified eyes off Thong's small brown neck, I think the views were good too. Everything was 'Wanderlust-style' Vietnam. There were green emerald fields, smoky distant bluish mountains and coffee-bean workers stooping in conical hats. But, between the views and me was the passing traffic. The bull-bars of which had become a focus for my frightened mind. Images of my body, smashed through to the blood and bone, projected themselves onto every approaching bumper.

But you love motorbikes, I reminded myself, you've ridden all over Greece and Turkey, spent endless wet Sundays spinning off-road monsters around muddy fields. Yes, I replied to myself, but then I had hold of the *bloody* handlebars.

And that was that really. When we stopped I asked Thong to go slower. He did try, but all the over-taking traffic seemed to taunt him. Plus, he wanted us to go quickly as there were so many other villages and waterfalls he wanted us to see before the end of the day. Eventually I explained to him we didn't want to see anything other than the pavement back in Dalat. He thought it was a bit odd. As did my friends, but I didn't care by then, I'd been 'outed', not as the go-anywhere-do-anything-with-anyone adventurer I'd like to have been, but as a common-or-garden control freak, and a somewhat chicken one at that.

Olivia Edward, 29 years old, Editor of Voyage, British, living in Shanghai

Favourite Hobbies: Off-road motorbiking, sailing, eating Sunday roasts and swimming in rough seas

Favourite Country: Guatemala

Favourite Book: Sheepshagger by Nial Griffiths

Other Publishing Experience: Various reviews for magazines and journals

58 VIETNAM: A LONG WAY TO GO

You think someone important is about to arrive when you land at Ho Chi Minh, or Saigon as many Vietnamese still like to call it. Thousands of people are outside the arrivals hall to wait for friends and family, or just to watch the comings and goings of these people with money on those clever flying machines.

In Ho Chi Minh there are probably fifty bikes for every one car, each jostling, swerving and avoiding the other. It's Sunday afternoon, and the day on which to be seen. Perched on one of the numerous Hondas will pass some of the most beautiful women you have seen in your life. Wearing long flowing Saffron dresses, with a matching bonnet tied just beneath the chin. For maybe just one afternoon a week, happy people are out showing themselves off in their Sunday best.

Ho Chi Minh's market is a feast for the eyes too. Piles of fruit and vegetables, eggs, chickens dead and alive; tee-shirts, electric drills, American binoculars and field compasses with a very new 1966 stamped on them; puppies, monkeys, cages of birds, and shoes made while you wait. If they had the money the Vietnamese would probably not be doing too badly - but therein lies the problem, for the Vietnamese are very poor people.

In the Old City houses built from wood and corrugated iron are often left half finished. Stone buildings crumble, their electricity supply erratic. Rubbish lies on street corners and children dodge the effluent as they play ball with empty Smarty tubes. And yet the Vietnamese are dignified and deeply hospitable people. A European face is still not usual in this country and walking along the street, or in the market, frequently draws a smile or a cheerful hello.

Vietnamese history has been a cruel one and they don't let you forget it. The American War Atrocity Museum is a deeply disturbing place. Here old American military hardware lies in the searing heat, their gruesome uses written on a nearby board. A bulldozer used to flatten suspect Vietcong-held villages, a plane used to spray the defoliant chemical 'Agent Orange', there is even a guillotine used by the French to quell colonial unrest - the wrong museum but the right impact.

And then inside are the photos of My Lai. In 1968 American troops, angered and humiliated by recent ambushes, went into villages to deal out terrible retribution on the village folk. The photo in front of me was of a group of terrified women and children standing by a ditch, moments before being shot by soldiers. One Court Martial eventually followed, a Lieutenant who was charged with the murders of 22 unarmed civilians. He was paroled shortly afterwards. I wonder if he tells his children what he did in the war.

Pay a pedal taxi driver a couple of dollars and he will show you the sights in passable English. Mine was keen to give me the complete history tour. I was more concerned about not giving him a heart attack. Even with the greatest respect for my pedalling friend, I have had younger taxi drivers showing me around, let alone cycling me in excess of 90 degrees of heat!

Ho Chi Minh drips in history. The Chinese influence is never far away. The statue of the Emperor Jade stands in his Pagoda maybe twenty feet tall, surrounded by hundreds of lit joss sticks. Their smoke rises to the roof like a thick fog. Their sweet-smelling incense lingers, and permeates the nose. At the end of a boulevard stands the Vietnamese Notre Dame, built by the French. Just opposite, the General Post Office. Inside, a huge hall like a railway station with a high vaulted ceiling. Desks surround its walls - letters to China, parcels for Europe, International Telephone Calls etc. And looking down on it all, a huge portrait of the man himself, Ho Chi Minh.

Back outside I get mobbed by a group of urchins, desperate to sell me a packet of ten postcards for one dollar. Hastily back onto the Cyclo virtually devoid of currency, my learned driver pedals me past the old US embassy, from whence the Ambassador departed in a bit of a rush in 1975. The building lies abandoned. Symbolically, a large tree trunk has grown up in front of the main door, rupturing the pathway and up into the porch. I have a feeling the Vietnamese are happy to leave it that way.

On my last night in Ho Chi Minh I took a pedal taxi down to the Saigon River. The time was 10.00pm and the streets were quiet, the silhouettes of buildings still until morning. A man in his office clothes was asleep in a closed doorway. The space was smaller than his body so his head and legs were cruelly buckled at right angles to the floor. Alongside the river floating restaurants were serving desserts. I sat at a small bar on the quay lit by a number of globes, which attracted thousands of frantic, suicidal insects. Across the river stood the great advertising hoardings of the West: Heineken, Philips, Fuji, Sony, their fluorescent colours reflected garishly in the water. A floating restaurant passed by with a live band. A tiny ferry set off to the other side of the river, and a young girl waved cheerfully to me as her boat disappeared into the darkness. It was an ideal scene - there was even a full moon.

In the years to come billions of dollars will have to be spent to rebuild war-torn Vietnam. And then there are electricity, water and health. Vietnam has a long way to go. Embargoes lifted, the country should begin to advance like the rest of SE Asia. My one real hope is that the kind Vietnamese people get the chance to develop and benefit from the future as well, for the past has not been a kind one. I wonder what my pedal taxi driver will make of that.

Jeremy Humphries, 42 years old, Film cameraman, England

Favourite Hobbies: Writing, painting, gardening

Favourite Country: Italy

Favourite Book: Birdsong by Sebastian Faulks

Other Publishing Experience: Selection of articles for magazines and newspapers, plans to write a novel

59 ON TOP OF THE WORLD

It is 6.00am. My Yoga class begins. I am teaching on the roof of a Tibetan nunnery, our new class venue. A rather large, soft, brown-furred, red-bottomed monkey reaches effortlessly to his toes and sits quite human-like beside me as if I am his kin, we probably do look much alike especially as I continue to contort my body into yogic postures. He sits close by me, reaching casually to play with his toes.

I am in the village of McLeod Ganj, home for many Tibetan refugees, and the place of residence of the Dalai Lama. The settlement nestles at the foot of the Himalayan mountain range in northern India. The village, surrounded by evergreen pine, is settled within a cradle of mountains that reaches up into the early morning skies. I am sharing the Yoga here with two other teachers: Vijay and François.

Vijay is a dark-skinned, southern Indian, with a slight build and extremely supple body. He has a strangely tribal bone structure giving him a very peculiar-shaped face; his motivation for teaching is a combination of spiritual calling and an insatiable desire for white women!

Then there is François, quietly spoken French accent, well sculptured with an elegant posture and strong male presence, a popular delight and motivation for our female Yoga students. Vijay, François and I share teaching and techniques with each other, and our students to come to daily practice.

Morning class is accompanied by the rising golden sun and the sweet angelic voices from the Gompa, the centre of a Tibetan Temple. The nuns sing harmonious mantras that drift up on the gentle breeze. They sit cross-legged on the temple floor in meditation, making mourning offerings of candles and water bowls to the Buddha. Between prayers they slurp and sip on salty-butter Tibetan tea, a local delight.

The nunnery is a way of escaping and surviving war torn Tibet, for young and older women who manage to flee the occupying Chinese regime. They take up renunciation: shave their heads and sometimes leaving their families behind them; it is their chance for freedom. These women remain in the nunnery clothed, fed and devoted to the teachings of the Buddha. A sense of sadness and loss in their eyes, but a feeling of gratitude and sweet innocence is to be seen in their smiles.

The class proceeds and our senses drift as soft silver-lined cotton wool clouds pass overhead, enwrapping snow peaked ridges, pink mountain tops and a new day lights up before us. We can hear the nuns giggle, curious and bewildered at this strange trio of white people contorting their bodies, as we practise our Yoga on the roof of the world.

Emily Dawson, 31 years old, Artisan, England

Favourite Hobbies: Singing, dancing and loving

Favourite Country: Bali

Favourite Book - I'Ching

Other Publishing Experience: A life time of journals

60 DOG BITES MAN

It was an unlikely setting to contract a fatal disease. As the early evening trade wind cooed through the palm fronds, the waves of the Sibuyan sea caressed the shore. It would have been desperately ironic if such soporific bliss spawned an agonising death.

There seemed no danger as we sat down to eat just yards from the bleached sand of the Philippine island of Boracay. But as I was served chicken with chilli and coconut, trouble lurked in the lean, starving shape of a local mongrel.

All I glimpsed was a flash of brown fur. Bonzo - as my girlfriend and I dubbed him - might have been Boracay born and bred, but he had a surprisingly international palate. To-day's *plat du jour* was Englishman's Leg.

It was a synchronised attack. As I bit into my chicken, so Bonzo's teeth punctured the skin beneath my right knee. And as coconut sauce dribbled down my chin, so his saliva mingled with my blood, trickling down my shin. I kicked out and he fled back to the shadows.

Now this was no snarling hound, no grizzled Rottweiler. But in a country where rabies is an everyday threat, I now had mongrel's saliva swirling around my bloodstream

Perhaps it was the mañana attitude that infects visitors to the tropics, perhaps it was the contented swell of a large meal and several San Miguels, but possible health repercussions didn't register. Friends examined the wound, said 'Ooh that's unlucky' and opened another beer. I too shrugged it off.

Until 2.00am that is. Then, as if starring in a fifties B-movie, I sat up wide-eyed, sheets clinging to my sweat-soaked chest. I'd had an unnerving flashback to a recent conversation with a tobacco farmer on the main island of Luzon.

After he'd been bitten on the buttock by a dog, the animal was captured, killed and analysed. It had rabies - and he'd endured a painful set of life-saving injections in his stomach. You die, he told me matter of factly, frothing at the mouth, your back arched with violent convulsions.

Boracay had a medical centre - all yellowing birth control posters, rusty syringes, buzzing flies - and a health worker. But he didn't inspire confidence when I visited next day. Yes, he'd known animal rabies on the tiny island, but never a human victim.

A quick look at the bite and he declared:

'No, you're fine.'

Just like that. Now I know you can tell a lot from a bite - in the neck or face, it will reach the brain faster - but his rapid-fire diagnosis struck me as a tad complacent. It was like studying someone's dick and declaring them AIDS-free. This is a disease transferred by a lick on a break in the skin for God's sake.

His next suggestion was absolute lunacy. Track Bonzo for a few days and if he avoided the sea catch and behead him, then send his brain for analysis. Not easy. Boracay had packs of Heinz-57 mongrels, none of which I'd seen doggy-paddling in the briny. Short of a canine massacre, I'd never find out which, if any, were infected.

Twenty-four hours later my girlfriend and I set off for neighbouring Panay, travelling by boat and ubiquitous Philippino bus: people on the roof, pigs in the luggage compartment, chickens in the aisle. Our destination? Kalibo. I'll let Lonely Planet describe its groovy attractions: *'A few kilometres south is Aklan Agricultural College. There are some interesting plant projects.'* Marvellous.

Surreal events were adding to my tension. Discovering I was from London, my motorised tricycle driver announced:

'Ah, yes, we hear it is not safe to drink the water there.'

Maybe, but the saliva's fine…

After an eleven hour journey I was eventually seen by a harassed doctor. She treated me with open derision. In a country where 45 out of every 1,000 children die before they're five, I was an overweight tourist expecting immediate attention for a dog bite.

'It could be rabid,' she said, examining the broken skin, 'But if locals get bitten, there's no treatment they can afford. Vaccine's £600. Pay and it's yours.'

Not a chance. And I'd no money left for an early flight back home. It was now two days since the bite and the clock was ticking. I was starting to fret.

Ignorance was fuelling my anxiety. I didn't know how long I'd got before treatment became ineffective. There was only one course of action for a fearless, pioneering, live-on-the-edge 30-year-old traveller who's in deep shit: call Mum and Dad.

Or his girlfriend's Mum and Dad. He was a South Manchester GP, and a veteran of the British army in Borneo - just the man for a South-East Asia health crisis. Minutes later I was connected from the chaos of Kalibo post office to the serenity of Cheshire.

A quick scratch of the head, check of the text books and it was good news. Very good news. Given I was bitten on my leg, he believed I'd be OK to get treatment immediately I returned nine days later. Even if Bonzo was rabid, the vaccine would save me. Relax.

And that's what I did, returning, slightly nervously to lengthy post-exposure treatment: vicious injections over several months in the muscley shoulder tissue; not, thank the Lord, my stomach. Each one involved mixing special water with a sample of the killer virus - I kept it in the fridge next to the yoghurt - producing a violently pink vaccine.

If I went away, I took it with me. One memorable injection was given by a Glasgow doctor on New Year's Eve. He appeared to have trouble focussing, sticking the needle somewhere around my elbow.

But I was fine. I still am. Bonzo, rabid or not, left an indelible mark on my leg and my memory. I recently read that one of Boracay's leading tourist attractions is roasted flying dog. I missed out last time, Bonzo. Revenge could be very, very sweet.

Ian Belcher, 42, Journalist, England

Favourite Hobbies: Running, cricket, movies, swimming, hiking

Favourite Country: Argentina

Favourite Book: Fools Rush In by Bill Carter

Other Publishing Experience: Articles in The Times, Guardian Weekend, Guardian, Observer, Sunday Telegraph, Jack, Eve etc

61 FOLLOW THAT NUN!

We were packed in like cattle and wishing for a seat after standing for a hot, sticky hour on an American school bus in Luzon, Philippines. You know the type: bright yellow, rickety, a shot suspension groaning with each pothole. On this kind of long, bumpy journey emotions run pretty high. You pray your rucksack is still fixed to the roof, you're stuck at someone's armpit level and you might be asked at any moment to hold someone's chicken.

A kind lady in a habit offered to share her seat with me. My friend and I swapped nervous glances - who wanted to sit next to this nun? I can't remember why we felt anxious (did she smell?), but I drew the straw to sit next to her.

We struck up a bond when we learned she had recently returned from secondment to a church in Mill Hill, about fifteen miles from where my travelling companion and I grew up. Suddenly I was her best friend and for the next few bumpy hours, (and two flat tyre episodes) I patiently listened to her stories about the Saints. Every now and then I would glance over at my friend who was quietly smirking to herself as she watched me enduring some stern preaching about how I should conduct my life. It smacked of our schooldays all over again!

We were on the first leg of our two-day bus trip to the spectacular rice terraces of Banaue, a contender for the eighth wonder of the world, and the pinnacle of our impromptu visit to the Philippines, one of the poorest countries in the world. Our overnight stop was a tiny village in the middle of nowhere. It was a gamble, and we arrived to find a couple of shacks, dirt-filled roads and frankly not a lot else.

It is in places like these that your travel guide becomes your trusted friend. Unless, that is, the village is of such little consequence that its description says little more than, 'you will find little more than a couple of shacks, dirt-filled roads and frankly not a lot else'. Not even a whisper on where to find water, let alone where to rest our heads. It was one of those moments when you try to look clued-up on the outside and on the inside you start swearing. Just a little bit. Okay a lot, but at least the nun couldn't hear!

Or could she? Because as dusk was approaching she too got off at our excuse for a bus stop and demanded to know where we were staying. She summed up our blank faces and feeble mutterings, took charge and told us to follow her. As she climbed into a dusty, egg-shaped bubble car attached to a motorcycle, we were commanded to jump into a similar 'vehicle' behind her.

This was a feat in itself. It was very possible that two girls, two large rucksacks weighing in at about 17kg apiece, plus one taxi driver would cause the contraption to keel over. Suddenly the scene became something out of a 'Carry On' film, further compounded when we instructed the driver, with a dramatic point forward, to:

'FOLLOW THAT NUN!'

Fifteen minutes and many potholes later we arrived at a missionary hospital, cool, serene and starkly white. We were led down disinfected corridors and paraded as 'The English Girls' to all the staff in the grand, brick building. We must have looked such a fright in our Thai fisherman trousers and dirty t-shirts.

Still uncertain of our night's accommodation, the nun then whisked us off in yet another type of rickshaw to meet the former Mother Superior. She lived in a bungalow on a plot of land with a barren garden comprising little more than black, volcanic soil. As we sat drinking tea on the porch with the sun setting, the contrast with the imposing missionary hospital could not have been more harsh.

Once we returned to the hospital, always being expected to pay for the nun's separate taxis, we struck gold. Her former secretary ran a lodge and was able put us up for a night so we piled over to Sue Ann's, where she made up some mattresses in a room for us. She sent out one son to buy a piece of fish (where from?!) and another for a crate of beer.

We were treated like royal guests, lavished with an authentic, home-cooked feast, with soup, chicken, potatoes and vegetables and of course the precious fish, which we ate together around the family table. After dinner we swapped stories on the veranda, drinking beer till the early hours of the morning. We could not have asked for more kind and entertaining people. Of all my travels that evening represents one of the most pleasurable local experiences of my life.

And the hospitality did not end there. At 5.00am, only a few hours after we'd turned in, a hot breakfast was forced upon us, before the eldest son took each of us in turn to a larger bus stop on his moped. Of course we left them money but it wasn't expected of us, such was their kindness.

It was almost a shame to leave. But we had rice terraces to see, tribespeople to meet, mountainous hairpin bends and landslides to contend with. Yet we knew we'd be safe; somewhere in a valley below a nun was praying for us. So when you next roll your eyes to heaven, be careful what you wish for - but if you are lucky, it might just turn out to be better than you expected.

Sophia Child-Villiers, 32 years old, Corporate Communications, England

Favourite Hobbies: Travelling, snowboarding, yoga, photography, cinema, modern art and working out how to make my millions!

Favourite Country: I like to think that I haven't visited my favourite country yet

Favourite Book: No one favourite but the London's A-Z is well thumbed

Other Publishing Experience: None but could become a potential hobby...

62 TITANIC OR TENEMENT?

At dusk in Chongqing's dock the Yangtze looks sleek and romantic. From the deck we watch the lights on the water below.

'Cheers!' says Luke, and we clink our shot glasses of Glenfiddich.

Passengers cheer and wave as we move out into mid-river, our ship's horn bellowing like a pregnant monster cow. I lean over the rail and study the exterior of our four-tier floating home for the next two days and nights. It looks impressive, a bit like a smaller Titanic.

Luke and I have booked a passage down China's longest river, mainly because by 2009 its main attraction, the Three Gorges, will be completely submerged by the creation of the Gezhou Dam - as will 13 cities, 140 towns and 1,352 villages. The Yangtze will become a 400 mile-long lake. We are to travel from Chongqinq in Sichuan province to Yichang, and we're not sure what to expect.

We share a second-class cabin with a Chinese family. The Granddad comes forward with a manic grin and introduces himself as Mr Ou Yang.

'I am a paediatrician,' he announces proudly. It turns out that's all the English he knows. We communicate with gestures and bad Mandarin, as we munch on French bread, camembert and duck liver paté (bought at a Carrefour in Chongqing!). The family crunches chicken and slurps noodles. Granddad chain smokes, and declines to try the paté.

At 5.00am we're shocked awake by a woman shouting over the Tannoy:

'We have docked,' she yells in Chinese, 'There's a small mountain to climb and a pagoda to...'

But Luke, bleary-eyed, cuts her off in mid-flow by slicing the wires of our cabin's speaker with his penknife. Granddad raises an approving thumb, and we all fall back into a hot sleep.

When we wake we're on the move again, heading for Wanxian. I'm amazed to see rows of dripping trousers, T-shirts and children's pyjama suits hanging from the light fittings on every deck.

This isn't the boat for deck tennis or shuffleboard. Instead, the women sit chatting amongst the hanging laundry, combing out their newly-washed hair. The Tannoy plays soaring music - punctured by the sounds of men spitting very loudly. Everyone hangs about in white vests smoking Double Happiness cigarettes, while little fat babies tip water on us from above. Not exactly the Titanic now - more like a New York tenement block.

The only other westerners we meet are two South Africans and a tattooed Englishman. Luke and I play backgammon, hang out with our Chinese family and walk the decks to take in different views. The Yangtze's banks are lined with flood markers charting the river's future steady climb up the mountain. Below most of the towns lie piles of rubble from destroyed buildings, while workmen build new flats and huge bridges higher up. Nearly two million people will be displaced by the dam, and the government offers them discounts on new flats and a choice of government jobs or cash settlements.

The water of the Yangtze is a churning, chocolate-orange swirl, big enough to swallow the noodle boxes and newspapers our fellow passengers have been chucking overboard continuously. That night we sleep with our side of the ship hard up against a luxury tourist boat. When the portholes of all the tightly-sealed, air-conditioned cabins are lit up the effect is magical, like gazing into a giant, living doll's house.

At six the following morning, in the light of a spectacular orange sunrise, we are treated to the first of the three gorges. Qutang Xia is the smallest and shortest gorge at 8km, but we still feel dwarfed by the sloping mountains. In the semi-darkness you can't see the flood markers and the river looks spruced and raging.

Our booking included a pre-paid trip up the Daning River. At 11.00am we are crammed into hot, tiny boats and subjected to a barrage of commentary from hand-held speakers. Among the rock formations, which our guide points out resemble various animals like dragons, pigs and - could that be a horse? - we spy a coffin, placed impossibly high up in a mountain cave by an ancient tribe. We're spooked as we admire the slim black box through our binoculars.

Half way upriver we disembark and walk to where market sellers lie in wait, offering fake antiques, old coins and fossils. Luke succumbs to a bird fossil, but later we see the identical item available at five other stalls. Granddad buys us a Coke and we sit on a stony beach in harsh sunlight, waiting an hour for our boats to pick us up. It is too long, even for the patient Chinese.

Back on the mother ship we are treated to the Wu and Xiling gorges. Wu Xia has cliffs on either side rising to over 900m, and Xiling Xia lasts for 80km. Both are imposing, slightly eerie and just as beautiful as we'd imagined.

Shortly before we dock we pass through the locks of the huge Gezhou Dam, to its construction site. There has been massive criticism of the dam - critics say it will destroy important cultural relics, tombs and temples, threaten species like the Chinese river dolphin, and place lives at risk where China has seen 3,200 dams burst since 1949.

But for most Chinese the dam spells progress, and they welcome it.

'With a history of poverty, many Chinese cannot afford to be precious about these things,' says Zhang Chen.

Destined to be the largest hydroelectric dam in the world, it will boost China's energy output by 10%, improve transportation links and help control the Yangtze summer floods, which kill thousands every year.

In darkness the site resembles a giant fun fair, with neon lights and unnaturally high cranes. The deck is more packed than ever before, and I stand at the forward end enjoying the scene and the cool air. I'm back in Titanic mode again, and not convinced I want to get off. It's hard to believe that within the next decade the river will change forever.

Caroline Sylge, 34 years old, Writer, England

Favourite Hobbies: Yoga, travel, eating out

Favourite Country: Namibia

Favourite Book: The Penguin Book of American Verse

Other Publishing Experience: Articles in newspapers and magazines

63 DOC ON WHEELS

Bloody nuns!

I jump onto the motorbike. The sun shimmers into evening after the full roast of day. No time to be embarking on a lone, three-day motorcycle journey. Especially not when my biking experience consists of a two-day course before I left the UK, plus a quick practice run round a field, but they have really pissed me off. I stamp on the starter pedal. (Splut.) Shit! So much for coming to Sierra Leone to save my soul - I never used to swear. That too is the nuns' fault. Hmmph! (Splutt-t-t-t-t.) Shit!

We can't rely on volunteers, they announced at the Board Meeting. Not the same commitment, they said. How dare they suggest I wasn't committed? Who ran their bloody hospital alone for four months when the rebels had chased everyone else away? Did one of them come to visit whilst I was on call twenty-four hours a day, seven days a week, with no other doctor in sight? (Splutt-t-t.) I even tried a nervous breakdown, but did they come to help? No. (Splutt-t-t.) Well I'm not spending another moment at Serabu - I'll go as far as the Mines tonight. Someone will feed me gin and chocolate. If I can get this damned bike started.

(Spluttt-t-t-t-t-t.) Yes! We're off!

I knock the visor down and lurch out of the hospital compound, my change of T-shirt and knickers, toothbrush, water bottle, anti-malarials and motorcycle tools (oh yeah?) strapped to the back. I wobble past the concrete corrugated iron-roofed buildings selling bananas and cigarettes on their verandas, then the mud huts with twisted palm leaf roofs and finally out into the palm trees and bushland. I weave in and out of huge puddles in the road, which steam from the afternoon downpour.

Three miles out of Serabu we join Mines' road, allowing me to surge up to a full 30mph. I'm free! I am going two hundred miles to visit the girl I met on the plane, the new Jane Goodhall they call her, to study chimps deep in the Salonean bush. Wow, real David Attenborough stuff. This is what coming to Africa is all about. An intrepid Girls Own Adventure heroine, that's me!

But first stop the Mines, to top up on petrol, gin, cheese and chocolate.

The short cut across the Mano River Bridge will save me fifty miles. I arrive just as the sun slips into hiding behind the bushes. It's very pretty in the evening glow. Rich green foliage crowding the bank, tumbling into the water whilst foaming white horses gallop down the exuberant river. Very attractive, but where's the bridge? I lift my visor. The road runs five or ten metres then vanishes under water. Shit. It'll be dark in half an hour and I don't have enough petrol to go the long way round. I'm not sure I even have enough petrol to get back to Serabu.

I edge the bike along a few metres. The water is just lapping over the edge of the bridge. It can't be that bad, there's only about fifty metres to cross. I get off and push.

At first my feet just gently splash in the water. Hey, this is OK. My feet aren't even getting wet. Then it laps at ankle height. Okay, my trainers will soon dry at the Mines. Then it creeps up over the front wheel and sucks at my shins. This is stupid - I'll have to go back. But I can't turn the bike round against the force of the river. I'll have to drop the bike. God, I can't do that! It isn't even my bike. I stand, paralysed, a third of the way across the river. What am I going to do? Why have I been so stupid? HELP!

Then in answer to my prayers a lad appears on the far bank. He waves and smiles. Thank God. I edge towards him. If I just keep going he can meet me halfway. It is at my knees now. Bloody hell. What is he doing? He just stands there, waving and smiling. Water splashes over my shoulder, my hair is wet. Oh God, I'll have to drop the bike, and turn round. No, how will that help? I am leaning against the bike at forty-five degrees into the current. I daren't let go now - the bike will knock me down.

I clench the handlebar tighter than ever and lean. I know about leaning into corners on a bike but this is ridiculous. Why isn't that boy coming to help?

Oh God, don't let me die. Not like this. Not doing something so stupid. And not when I've spent the last hour of my life cursing your daughters-of-virtue. At least let me die saving my patients from hordes of rebels or something. Not like this. Well, not at all really. HELP!!

I keep pushing and leaning into the current. For the first time in my life I'm glad of my eleven-and-a-half stone. Why doesn't that bloody boy do something?

Halfway! I am halfway. I keep pushing. I don't have to lean quite as much, the water is subsiding - I am going to make it. I come out the other side, and the water drains from the wheels. YES!

'Do ya, Dr. Em, you go gi me lift?' asks the boy with a cheesy grin.

'WHAT?! Bugger off!' I splutter.

Give him a lift? Never raised a hand to save me, and he wants a lift? There I was, nearly swallowed up by the surging river and taken directly to Hell, and he just waited to see if I lived or not so he could ask me for a lift? Bloody hell. I mount my bike, woman and machine now bonded by adversity, and jump on the starter pedal.

Did I seriously think it would start? I push the bike the final two miles to the Mines.

Emily Joy, 41 years old, Doctor, Scotland

Favourite Hobbies: Eating, talking, walking, writing, painting (and hopefully sports again, three small children allowing)

Favourite Country: Scotland

Favourite Book: 101 Dalmatians

Other Publishing Experience: One book - Green Oranges on Lion Mountain and currently writing 2 others

64 LIFE'S A BYTCH

I used to love driving. I was like a dog with its saliva-covered snout hanging out the window...loved it! All that changed however when I returned to live in Southern California. It's my own fault really. I haven't quite mastered the art of driving in Southern California. People make virtual lounges out of their SUVs. When I'm stuck in traffic, which is pretty much all the time, I can often watch someone else's car TV from behind my steering wheel. It's sort of like reading over someone's shoulder on the Underground, only you're in the privacy of your own vehicle and they don't actually know that you're doing it. Perhaps if I would just conform and convert my vehicle into my primary residence like everybody else, I would embrace the nightmare that is driving in Southern California.

At least somebody was thoughtful enough to create the drive-thru. When I first returned here I cursed the drive-thru to high Heaven. In fact, if you turn to the Seven Deadly Sins section of the Bible and look up 'Sloth', you will most likely find an illustration of an In-N-Out Burger drive-thru. I loathed the drive-thru when I first arrived here, yet now, I worship it. One can get a burger, shake, money, milk, eggs, and cigarettes with a mere tap of the gas pedal. Every day I dream of leaving California, but then I think:

'How will I manage without the drive-thru?'

Not only is it amazingly convenient, it's educational, perplexing, and it keeps us questioning life and our existence. For example, I enjoy the challenge of trying to decipher the whining screech coming out of a loudspeaker disguised as Coco the clown. And the guesswork that goes into wondering if they actually got my order right. It makes the journey to the pick-up window downright exhilarating.

The bank drive-thru is a bit more cut and dried. First of all, there's no Coco-the-clown speaker. It's just your average run-of-the-mill cash point. The biggest challenge is choosing a language:

English or Español. Lately however, the odd Chinese character has begun to sneak in. So I now have a choice of English, Español, or Chinese. The bank drive-thrus are always upping the ante on you with their language choices.

Very recently I was thrown a curve ball in the form of Tagalog.

'Tagalog,' I kept repeating to myself.

I've been saddled with tagalongs. I've even been a tagalong myself. But this was Tagalog. So I decided to do my bank transaction in Tagalog and see where it got me, which wasn't very far. The screen was filled with some sort of cryptic code. Was this the mysterious Tagalog showing itself? All I wanted was to satisfy my curiosity and get twenty bucks. But the cars behind me were getting itchy, revving their engines. So I pressed the Tagalog word for 'cancel' and waited for the language menu to reappear. Instead the sound of marbles dropping onto a glass table blasted out of the speaker. This was Tagalog I was hearing. The guy behind me honked. So I reverted to English, got my twenty bucks and drove off before I was lynched by an angry mob of suburban motorists.

The Tagalog discovery piqued my curiosity. And I found myself making unnecessary trips to the bank drive-thru just to see if any other new curve balls were being added to the language display, but the choices remained English, Español, Chinese, and Tagalog. Eventually my brother informed me, in his 'everybody knows that, you numbskull' voice, that Tagalog is actually Filipino. And pretty soon Tagalog became an everyday occurrence, a normal part of living in Southern California, like traffic jams, road rage, and Mexican food.

My drive thru lifestyle remained numbingly calm until one day, out of the blue, WA-BAM. It sideswiped me when I least expected it: Hmoob. Just say that to yourself a few times.

Hmoob.

I definitely wanted to know what Hmoob was all about. If it was up there on the screen, then obviously I was the last to know about it. Just as I was about to press the Hmoob display, the car behind me honked. It was the same guy as before, the ringleader of the suburban lynch mob. Before I could even say Hmoob, he had sidled right up next to my driver's side window, staring at me with piercing slits for eyes and said in a low gravel:

'Keep it movin' sister.'

I decided to go home and do some Hmoob research on my own time before I got my tyres slashed.

Thanks to Google, the drive-thru computer research centre, I was able to slouch in my chair all afternoon and read about Hmoob. I found out that it is the language of the Hmong people, refugees of Laos and Vietnam. How did I manage up to now without that information? I also learned that they don't have a proper written language, though apparently enough Hmoob exists to withdraw twenty bucks from the bank, which is a good thing.

I noticed too that the Hmongs use the letter Y very liberally, both in their own language and ours. For example, one Hmong American neatly bridged the gap between the ancient Hmong and modern American cultures by writing:

'Life is a bytch'.

I can't argue with the sentiment. However I do wonder if it's even more of a bitch when you spell it with a 'y'. Imagine the problems - and the massive achievement - involved in getting a totally unwritten language onto cash points throughout Southern California. It makes the Tagalog challenge look like a pushover.

It is weighty and diverting issues like these which enliven my day and explain my drive-thru addiction. Maybe life is not such a bytch in Southern California. At least it isn't Wysconsin.

Deirdre Wolf, 31 years old, A bit of a Jack Horner with a finger in a few pies, USA

Favourite Hobbies: Writing, snowboarding, playing the violin and self-deprecation

Favourite Country: England

Favourite Book: The Anarchist Cookbook and anything by Dr. Seuss

Other Publishing Experience: My Masterpiece which is collecting dust somewhere and stories for the local paper

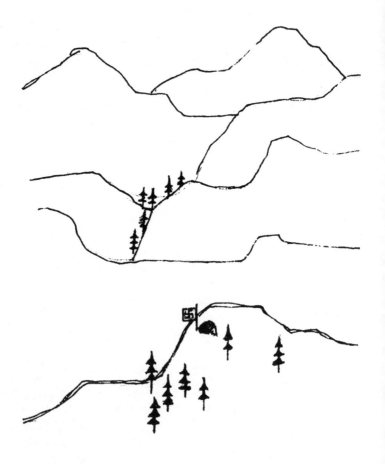

65 THE EAGLE'S LAIR

The name Berchtesgarten has become synonymous with Hitler's mountain retreat near the Austro-German border, though in fact the Fuehrer's Berghof chalet was in the smaller village of Obersalzburg, where he lived in Baronial splendour, playing despotic host to world leaders, including the sadly deluded Chamberlain in 1938. All were impressed with Herr Hitler's new valley which could be seen laid out below his gigantic picture window, his beloved Untersberg mountain in the background.

Adolf Hitler rented a house in Obersalzburg and liked it and its view of the Untersberg so much he bought it off the owners in 1932. He actually paid cash money for it - 40,000 gold marks - probably the last time he paid for anything instead of nicking it.

Gradually the lair of the wolf became so attractive to other Party members and Reich officials that every house in the village was bought by Nazis. Bormann, Speer, Goering - all had residences here, and over a billion marks was spent on the construction of buildings, Stormtrooper barracks and tunnels. By the beginning of the war not a single house in Obersaltzburg was still occupied by its original owners, and by the end of the war practically none remained standing - the R.A.F. bombed the shit out of it on April 25th 1945.

We didn't go to Obersalzburg because there's nothing to see - all the official buildings and Nazi chalets have gone, so too the network of tunnels and arsenals built into the mountain. It would have become a shrine to nasties, so it was wiped clean.

What we had come to see was the Eagle's Nest - Hitler's eyrie perched unfeasibly atop the Kehlstein alp, 6,000 feet up above the village. It sounds, as it was no doubt meant to, rather romantic - the lonely great leader ruling the world from his Wagnerian mountain fortress, impregnable and omnipotent - but the reality, as always, is somewhat less theatrical.

Assorted Nazi *Obergruppentoadies* decided to build a fiftieth birthday present for their Fuehrer on top of the alp - it would prove the might of German engineering and willpower, labour was cheap and expendable, and it would get them a billion brownie points. The result *was* a triumph of engineering and deadline-beating (not more than a hundred workers died during construction) but Hitler hardly ever went there - he was afraid of heights.

You can't drive up to it - the single lane road is spectacularly narrow and vertiginous - so you gather at a car park and bus terminal half way up the mountain, and catch a shuttle. It's worth the trip just for the bus ride up the hill. It is difficult to believe how it could have been built sixty years ago, and impossible to believe it could be built today. Several miles long, there's not a straight bit longer than twenty yards. Clinging to the cliff face, ducking in and out of tunnels, twisting and turning like a snake, the road is quite the hairiest I've ever been on.

Eventually it arrives at a small plateau at about 5,500 feet, where you get off. So as to preserve the outline of the mountain top, and no doubt for added security, they blasted straight into the rock and put in a lift - the only way up. You pass through a stone arch (with 1938 engraved into the keystone) and immediately pass into movieland - *The Guns of Navarone, Where Eagles Dare, Indiana Jones*, take your pick.

The long stone-lined and marble-floored corridor is damp with condensation and lit with small yellow bulbs in brass housings. It slopes gently upwards to a circular, domed ante-chamber where there are a pair of huge bronze doors - the lift. Inside it's the original lift, with brass and mahogany fittings and mirrors. This is getting very creepy indeed - what have *these* walls heard? Four hundred feet higher, the doors open into the stone building, and you are instantly hit by the smell of warm cabbage and roast something in gravy. Yes, it's a restaurant. Well you've got to cater for the masses who've made the pilgrimage up the Alp.

The original building still stands, but every corner of it smells of cabbage, so we go outside onto the stone terraces. Wow. This really is very high indeed. On three sides the cliffs simply disappear beneath you and all you can see is the valley floor 4,000 feet below. To the west is the beautiful Koenigsee lake and to the north the Untersberg, with the summit of which you are now level. Beyond is the smudge of Salzburg on the horizon.

You can climb up a path on the fourth side, further up the mountain, and turn to look back at the Eagle's Nest framed against its impossibly breathtaking 270 degree view. There's a large wooden cross and a cairn of stones at the top of the path. It would be nice to think it had some small meaning in this unearthly place, but it's a memorial for the Alpine Climbing Association or some group of that ilk. I suppose a cross large enough to address the bigger issue would have to be as tall as the sky.

We have a basic lunch out on the terrace, and just before we go I notice a covered stone balcony or terrace to the left, one wall completely open and looking out westwards. There's nobody there so I quietly walk along, looking out to my left at the amazing view. I suddenly stop cold and open my copy of the brochure I'd bought at the shop and flicked through during lunch. There, on page nineteen, was a black and white picture of the Fuehrer with the French Ambassador. It was grainy, but it was quite clear that I was now standing on the exact same spot, on the same unchanged and undamaged flagstone that Adolf Hitler stood on exactly sixty years ago.

Time to go, I think.

Jonathan Booth, 44 years old, Internet video pioneer, England

Favourite Hobbies: Movies, cards, golf, cricket

Favourite Country: England

Favourite Book: The Hobbit

Other Publishing Experience: One book - The European Job, numerous film reviews and trade articles

66 ST DENNIS THE BLESSED

Paris is a city of many saints - St. Germain, St. Honoré and St. Michel, to name but a few. Nominated but yet to be officially beatified is the Antipodean saint of Paris, St. Dennis the Blessed.

Arriving at 6.00am at Charles de Gaulle airport the French-speaking world is a frightening place. I felt more culture shock there on first arriving than I did on landing in Africa or Asia.

At our moments of greatest need we Australians seek each other out intuitively even when emphatically *not* wearing bush hats strung with corks. Sean approached Kat and me at the baggage carousel unhesitatingly, with this anxious but friendly opening gambit:

'Do you know where you're going, mate?'

I gathered that this Australian also felt alien in the kingdom of the Franks, and together we pondered maps, currency and transport options.

Using the same extra-sensory perception system, another figure in the crowd turned to us. Around his neck he wore a small, silver surfboard, a symbol of high church Australian worship. Looking back at that moment, I feel as if even then he gave off a faint but perceptible aura.

Dennis, as he introduced himself, was an Australian living in Paris, while his mother, shortly to arrive, was a Frenchwoman living in Australia. Dennis quickly divined that we were lost in this strange land, and offered to transport us back to his abode and orientate that grand city for us.

The First Miracle of salvation and generosity.

Under such hallowed guidance we journeyed into the city of the ancient Parisii, and were amazed by the scale, the architecture, the French-ness of which we had previously only dreamed.

How I remember the glorious 11th arrondisement. A narrow staircase led us to his humble home, at that time not yet honoured with a commemorative plaque. This was also the *pied à terre* of Elisabeth the Virgin. Arisen from her slumbers she appeared as an immaculate vision, flawless in hair, face and figure. She silently surveyed the lost flock of Australians gathered by the good shepherd, strode to the cupboard, poured a large glass of cognac and swallowed it in one gulp. Thereafter she greeted us in a composed and friendly manner.

Elisabeth was the Second Miracle.

In a stupendous welcome to Paris, Dennis produced a full French breakfast of café, baguettes, croissants, pastries and *confiture*. The Feeding of the Masses. The Third Miracle.

He then sent us out into this brave new world under his spiritual and corporeal guidance, laden with information on where to locate lodgings, change money and eat, and how to contact him at his place of employ, a bar off the Champs-Elysées.

The next evening we visited this haunt of publicans and sinners to witness the Fourth Miracle: a bottomless well of sustaining alcoholic beverages provided for us by Dennis (hallowed be thy name!). This was coupled with a firm refusal on his part to accept the financial tribute we offered in exchange for all this bounty. Wise men have told us that in Paris it requires great riches to partake of the fruits of fermentation.

St Dennis, thou art truly the Blessed One.

Steve Kelleher, 37 years old, Australian government, but always on leave, Australia

Favourite Hobbies: Bushwalking, reading, sleeping, boomerang throwing

Favourite Country: Laos

Favourite Book: One Crowded Hour by Tim Bowden

Other Publishing Experience: Some in-house articles and a few paragraphs in Lonely Planet newsletters

67 BORDER HOLD-UP

Only once have I seen a grown man fall flat on his face from a standing position. He landed with a much uglier noise than I expected, but I smiled and felt a strong sense of relief. For the first time in almost five hours my shoulders unclenched, and I was released from panicked images of a holiday turned dangerously sour. For a moment the squalid little border town that marks the end of the river route into Guatemala from Mexico seemed almost appealing.

It all started early that morning. A boneshaking taxi took us from our hotel in Palenque to the departure point on the river. It was a small hut beside a long brown puddle.

The trip down river was hot. There were flies. The boat was long and narrow, with someone at the front, to fend us off rocks, and another at the back to jazz the throttle occasionally. Besides we three English, there were a couple of Americans, a German, and a very pale Swiss with more sweat on his forehead than was warranted by the temperature. He was ill, unhappy, but tied to an itinerary he didn't have the initiative to suspend. No one talked much, besides one of the Americans, a fiftyish grey-bearded man wearing linen.

We approached the Guatemalan border town just as the sun was disappearing but even that generous light didn't make it look anything other than a crap little shacksville. There was a motel built on stilts by the riverbank, with walls of plyboard and a flat roof. It was a shit hole we would have to endure until such time as the bus showed up to drive us to the more touristic destination of Tikal. But that didn't seem so daunting that a few local beers wouldn't help smooth the time along.

We were greeted off the boat by the man whose face would later crunch onto the decking with a gristly thud. He wore cream trousers and a white sports coat, and he politely directed us onto the benches lining the hotel's terrace. It felt welcoming. When we were all seated he identified himself as the *Alcalde*, the guy who ran the town. We

229

all produced our passports and he began a tour of inspection.

The Swiss patient wheezed his identity and tried to look like someone who was well enough to be granted entry. But his illness was unmistakable, and he was packed off to a hotel room to recover. Then he spoke briefly to the Americans and the German in clipped tones, a parody of efficiency.

It was the summer of 1994 and England had failed to qualify for the World Cup finals. Again. I was well past feeling aggrieved. It just meant we were spared further excuses for serial underperformance. Our new host, however, was still relishing the fact of England's failure. Now was his chance to unburden himself of much suppressed hostility.

There is a direct correlation between the importance you attach to your passport and your distance from home. Sitting on that terrace, being taunted by an increasingly sinister Guatemalan mayor, made me feel more protective of it than ever before. Especially when he said that since we were no good at football, he was going to keep all three English passports. This wasn't somewhere I wanted to spend any more time than was strictly necessary. The mood quickly changed from one in which the group was collectively humouring a pathetic micro-potentate to one in which something potentially uncomfortable was developing.

'You will have to wait,' he taunted us. 'The rest can leave when the bus arrives. But you wait.'

Then he left for his office. We looked at one another. The German guy frowned in the way he thought we thought he should frown. The younger American looked sympathetic. And the elder American said:

'This is shit.'

And then he revealed that he had lived in Guatemala for ten years or so, and that petulant border episodes like this could turn into something more than a comic interlude for the travel diary.

'You need to get your passports back quickly,' he said, 'and I don't think you've got the first idea where to start, right?'

'Right,' we said pitifully.

'Shit,' he said again.

He disappeared off to the mayor's office, where in the course of the next three hours he consumed enormous quantities of locally-produced alcohol on our behalf. He returned from time to time as if to register the gradual deterioration in his speech.

'I think he's softening,' he would say, before disappearing again. Meanwhile, we sat in a state of confusion, premature gratitude, and intense anxiety. Time passed slowly. The bus would come eventually. But the fate of our passports remained unclear. Until eventually, the American rolled back onto the terrace waving all three of them at us.

'Here you go,' he said in many more syllables than the sentence required. We took the passports gratefully.

But within minutes there were sounds from the mayor's office. Stumbling footsteps approached. A body banged against thin walls. There were some slurred wailings. Our relief disappeared and new fears surfaced. The mayor joined us, swaying, and this time he was waving a pistol.

'You English bastards,' he slavered. And then all the drinking paid its dividends. His next step brought his head into brutal contact with a hardwood pillar in the middle of the terrace. The body wobbled for a minute and then, slowly, it tilted forwards, picked up speed, and finally went crashing towards the floor. Bang. And it was still. Still for at least the hour and a half before the bus finally arrived in the very early hours of the morning. Who knows how much longer.

It was light when we made it to Flores, the lakeside town that's a launch pad for Tikal. The elder American - still nameless - complained of an epic hangover and we reminded him of our gratitude. Then he disappeared and we found a room to stay.

Terence Henry, 32 years old, Lawyer, England

Favourite Hobbies: Sport particularly football, reading

Favourite Country: Thailand

Favourite Book: Lord of the Rings

Other Publishing Experience: Various articles for magazines

68 LEAVING TIBET

We are leaving Tibet, heading into China on the back of a truck - three Westerners, ten Tibetans and a baby. We have two drivers, Mohamed, older and experienced, and Jigme his young apprentice. Although it's July, high summer, it begins to get cold. During a pee stop I put my second pair of trousers on top of the first, my long underwear underneath both.

Soon road works begin. We are forced off the road into wet grooves, jolting over stones and sliding through mud, crossing streams, climbing rocky inclines, improvising a detour. We are bumped nearly to death. The Tibetans are quiet, patient, accepting. Not a peep from the baby. The Westerners fidget, chew biscuits, groan over bumps.

Suddenly we're in the depths of an arctic winter. We're dismally unprepared for the weather. Nobody wants to sit in the cab; though warmer, it's acutely uncomfortable. I'm the smallest so I volunteer; besides I'm so cold that heat at any cost seems a blessing. And the back of the truck isn't exactly the Ritz. But although the cab is warmer, there's no space for my blood to circulate. I'm beset by pins and needles.

The cab is crammed with tools, boxes, bags, rags, food and cigarettes. The seat is covered by a rancid sheepskin. Whenever the driver changes gears I'm prodded either by his elbow or the gear lever. The drivers are cheerful and friendly, but have one major flaw - they insist on force-feeding me.

First they present a brown and yellowish delicacy, some kind of biscuit I assume, hopefully part chocolate. It turns out to be a lump of yak meat. When I bite into it the yellow, pure fat, congeals on the roof of my mouth. The brown, far from being chocolate, is tough, sinewy, unchewable. It's like eating leather laced with lard. However, I have no choice but to swallow. Later the driver sniffs the meat, wrinkles his nose in disgust and flings it out the window. It's gone off. I instantly feel poisoned.

While eating we ascend into mountains patchy with ice and snow and swept by freezing winds - a bleak ravaged landscape, the dark side of the moon. There is no humanity here. Again and again we're forced off the disintegrating road into rutted mud, swerving between rocks and ditches, charging at streams, bumping so violently my eyes are knocked against my skull. Periodically the engine gives up.

Mohamed is our salvation. He knows exactly what to do and eventually we lurch forward. Suddenly tents made from yak skins appear. I remember someone telling me that during the summer months the herdsmen sleep outdoors in yak-hair blankets and that young children go naked. I can't decide if this thought makes me warmer or colder.

For brief moments we encounter paved road. It's like driving on satin. My internal organs reorganize, grunting their way back into place - until the next onslaught. Despite the strain of keeping the truck moving, despite the agony of making repairs with numbed fingers, the drivers never lose their humorous view of things. A routine develops. Each time Mohamed spots a particularly wretched patch of road, he sighs a deep 'Ah yah', like a vast lament and I sigh a wailing 'Ah-yah' in sympathetic response, followed by a bleating 'Ah-yah' from Jigme. We have occasion to sigh many 'Ah yahs' together.

By the second day I'm wearing almost all my clothing: two tee shirts, long underwear, two pairs of trousers, three pairs of socks, a glittery Indian blouse, a tie-dye shirt, a sarong, a towel, a kerchief, my peacock shawl, and of course my Tibetan boots, but I'm so cold it's as though I'm naked. After a pre-dawn pee stop, which includes breakfast (tea from a thermos and damp biscuits) we return to the truck. But alas, it won't start. It's too cold. The drivers crank the engine again and again, but it refuses to catch. I'm banished from the cab. The seat has to be removed to get at the tools. I jump up and down to keep warm but my fingers and toes soon become numb. A dismal dawn chisels through the night and in the grey light I feel even colder.

To keep from freezing to death, I jog down the road, beating my arms like a broken bird. The surroundings are so forbidding, that I run back to the truck, relieved to see that the drivers are still alive. They crank the engine until they finally give up, exhausted. There is nothing I can do except freeze. From somewhere, Mohamed produces a blow-torch. He lights it, I think to warm their hands. To my horror he places it next to the engine, to heat it. I panic. I'm convinced we're going to explode into flames.

Should I wake the others? By the time I decide to save their lives, the blow-torch has disappeared. A truck comes to pull us. I'm invited back into the cab, wondering if burning to death is better than freezing. At least it's warmer. The engine starts. It's 7.00am, cloudy and very cold. A raven flies by, black against the snow. It begins to snow. A new day on the road begins.

Flat tyre. The drivers repair it while I freeze. They return to the cab in possession of two jars of preserved apples or pears; they look the same. Jigme pierces a piece of fruit with a screwdriver smeared with engine grease. I'm eating a noodle mixture from a plastic container. He offers me some fruit. I decline. Thinking I'm just being polite, he plops several pieces, pierced with grease, into my noodles. I'm starving and eat the lot. If the rotten yak meat didn't do me in, I guess this won't either.

At eight that night, the ordeal from hell is over. We've arrived. We embrace the drivers. Our final 'ah-yah' is a huge exhalation of warmth and affection. The truck pulls away without us.

Niema Ash, Ageless, Writer, England

Favourite Hobbies: Travelling, also love, life and the pursuit of happiness

Favourite Country: Morocco

Favourite Book: W.B. Yeats's poetry, also Catcher In The Rye

Other Publishing Experience: Touching Tibet and Travels with my Daughter (both by Eye Books) aside from many short pieces, stories, articles, etc

69 THE BANK ROBBERS

When the sloop *Luck-be-a-Lady* sailed for France on the Friday evening, no Jolly Roger flew at the masthead. We were nevertheless something of a motley crew.

Owner, Mike, had built a successful advertising agency. The rest of us were beholden to him one way or another. Ashby was his accountant, who periodically slapped the boat's hull and said: 'Paid for by the Inland Revenue!'

Ben was formerly one of London's hottest copywriters, but his creative flair dried up as his alcohol consumption travelled in the opposite direction. Four months ago Mike and Ben agreed to part company, a much-used euphemism. Mike had been not ungenerous, but Ben's credibility was running out as fast as his money. He badly needed a job, but dare not say so. He resented his dismissal, but dare not show it.

Frank was a stock character film actor, who for years played minor comic or criminal roles in British films. You'd recognise his face instantly. In the autumn of his career Frank featured in a long-running TV campaign, recently ended, for Mike's biggest client.

Last, youngest, uninvolved with Mike professionally, was me, Jim. I built hand-made furniture outside High Wycombe, I was Mike's cousin, and handy about a boat.

The Channel crossing by night was enjoyable but uneventful. Sea calm, following wind, full moon, a doddle. A leisurely morning in Cherbourg, a light lunch, then we'd catch the afternoon tide and claw our way up to Honfleur.

But first we should top up our Euros. Our preferred restaurateur for tonight's lobster supper didn't take plastic.

When you create a kitty you all put in the same, so Mike and Ashby held back to allow Frank to set the pace. But Ben, being Ben, must keep up appearances:

'Thirty quid each?'

Agreed all round, though a year before we'd done fine on half that. So Frank appointed himself treasurer, and collected our English money. Three of us paid up somewhat ruefully.

Mike and Ashby went back to the boat, and we three strolled into the Crédit Lyonnais. The bank was fairly busy, and Frank had to queue for the paperwork, then took the yellow slip to the *Caisse* to collect the money.

Ben and I sat down at the central table, until Frank came over clutching a big fistful of Euros. He made an actorly flourish of counting out the money onto the table, dealing out three little piles:

'Twenty for Ben, twenty for Jimmy, twenty for Frank. Forty for Ben, forty for Jimmy, forty for…'

At this point both the acting and the dealing stopped dead. Frank snatched up all the banknotes and hissed at us urgently:

'Everybody out!'

He then headed for the door at warp speed. Startled, Ben and I followed, both conscious that Frank had distributed 120 Euros, yet the fat bundle had not even begun to shrink. We got outside to see Frank halfway to the harbour, and actually trotting.

By the time Ben and I got aboard, Mike and Ashby were already more in the picture than we were.

'Ah-hah,' said Mike as we stepped down into the small saloon:

'Here come Butch and Sundance'.

Counted three times, it was undeniable that in exchange for his £150 yellow slip, Frank had been handed 2250 Euros, or £1500 odd.

'What do we do now?' asked Ben very carefully.

'Get that engine started, and cast off,' urged Frank, aggressively.

'You're joking,' said accountant Ashby, 'We have to return it, of course.'

'I am not,' said Frank, 'I mean it'. He looked ready to fight over it.

Ben looked less confident than usual. In work, a £300 windfall was nothing. But 'resting'?

'Mike?' he said, looking for leadership. Our Skipper shook his head.

'Up to you blokes,' he said. The money meant nothing to him, but he was aware that three of us were not finding it that easy to keep the potatoes arriving on the table.

'Come on, Mike' said Ashby, indignant, 'Quite apart from the moral issue, if we don't take that back we may all end up in the dock together. It isn't worth it.'

Ben tried another tack:

'What do you think five Frogs would do in our place? I bet they'd enjoy screwing the *anglais*...'

Mike looked at me:

'Come on, Jim, you might have the casting vote. What should we do?'

I hesitated. My head and heart were with Ashby, but my hip pocket was with Frank and Ben. Furniture was in recession, so retailers weren't buying. Again.

'How would it be' I said slowly, 'if we simply carry on with our agreed plan: make ready, and sail with the afternoon tide' (I looked at my watch) 'in about an hour's time? Either they catch us and we play surprised, stupid innocents. Or they don't, in which case we become the men who took the Crédit Lyonnais at Cherbourg, and dine out on it for life.'

'The judgement of Solomon,' said Mike, who with hindsight maybe planned to refund the bank secretly, thus giving each of us a small, unrefusable (because covert) handout.

Nobody either agreed or disagreed. My compromise was tacitly accepted.

The next hour passed very slowly.

We were on deck, jib attached but not hoist and motor running, when we saw the small boat move slowly round the harbour. A stocky, sweating, middle-aged farmer-figure rowed, while the bank clerk who had cashed Frank's yellow slip stood precariously in the bows, peering at every boat.

Frank gave a brilliant performance. An idiot English. No sense, less French. Didn't understand these new Euros. Our ill-gotten loot was rowed away. Two very relieved Frenchmen, and no apology for us.

But you've got to hand it to the French. Here was a prosperous, middle-aged, probably lifelong customer who'd signed away £1,500 and been handed £150. So how do they appease his natural anger? They say 'Go and find your money,' and send him rowing round the harbour on a hot afternoon. He probably had to pay for the boat.

Jim Coverley, 37 years old, Director, England

Favourite Hobbies: Sailing, cricket

Favourite Country: Ireland

Favourite Book: Any by Patrick O'Brien

Other Publishing Experience: None

70 HALFWAY TO HEAVEN

Our aeroplane is five minutes from its late afternoon landing in Paro, Bhutan. Since the airport is perched at an altitude of 7000 feet, the thinning tufts of clouds still captivate me, offering hide-and-seek glimpses of steep mountains on either side of the plane. Women stoop in small rice paddies below. They're close enough to see the vivid colours of their *kiras*, Bhutan's traditional clothing. Children wave enthusiastically, chasing the plane's shadow and shouting something that looks friendly.

We've heard that a safe arrival in Paro takes a skilled aviator, so it's a good time to remind ourselves that miracles are known to happen here.

The Kingdom of Bhutan is a world unto itself, nuzzled in the eastern Himalayas, north of India and south of Tibet. It's not just mountainous, it's virtually *all* mountain. Druk Air, with its entire fleet of two planes, is the only way to get there. It's also the only airline to fly over eight of the tallest peaks in the world, then land on a runway that's reportedly the longest flat stretch in the entire country.

The word *druk* means dragon. Bhutanese call their country *Druk Yul,* the Land of the Thunder Dragon. It's one of the world's biodiversity hot spots, with an estimated 165 mammal and 600 bird species. More than 70% of the Kingdom is forested. Its giant peaks have never been explored by westerners and are considered home to the deities, so climbing them is officially prohibited. Bhutan is so protective of its environment that plastic bags are illegal. Killing an endangered black-necked crane results in life imprisonment.

The King of Bhutan, His Royal Majesty Jigme Singye Wangchuck, is internationally respected for his focus on what he calls 'Gross National Happiness.' This is not a cute tourist theme, but a set of platforms on economic health, environmental preservation, cultural promotion and good governance. His Kingdom is relatively small, measuring 180 miles long and 100 miles wide, a land mass about the size of Switzerland. Although there are a few roads, much of the country can be reached only by footpath. Most of Bhutan's estimated 650,000 citizens are subsistence farmers scattered in remote valleys narrowly wedged between steep ridges. The average annual income is $500 US.

We have come here to witness a culture that straddles an improbable crevasse between the 17th and 21st centuries. Drawn to high mountain passes where prayer flags are planted in auspicious locations and where invocations are reportedly heard best by Himalayan gods and goddesses, we each have our own personal prayers for this challenged world. I'm eager to liberate mine.

Once we deplane, I touch the tarmac with a sigh of gratitude. Our entrance is already obscured by monsoon clouds - not the angry, hit-and-run variety, but more of the what's-the-hurry, drooling kind. They hang low on the mountains like gauze petticoats, seductively inviting an upward look.

Gradually I become aware of something soft and relaxing touching me, like fingertips on my jaw. It's the silence. No traffic, no leaf blowers, and - blessed be - no car stereos. There is literally nothing to hear but the wind and the birds. An *aficionado* of quiet, I am now halfway to heaven.

It's easy to like the first Bhutanese we meet, such as the immigration official who declares our visas expired last week. We show him our itinerary. *No problem*, he shrugs, extending our legal time with a proper stamp and without fee. Leaving customs, we're greeted by a man wearing a *gho*, something resembling a rather colourful knee-length bathrobe with rolled-up sleeves. He holds a sign with our all seven of our names, an especially charming gesture since there are exactly seven tourists in the entire airport. *I am Wangdi. I am your guide.* Wangdi bows and introduces us to our driver, whose name sounds exactly like Shut Up. We laugh, Wangdi laughs, Shut Up laughs.

We're shuttled to a hotel in a blue pine forest amongst flower paths, and given tiny keys on huge brass key chains heavy enough to double as weapons. Our next days are spent exploring remarkable fort-monasteries called *dzongs,* shopping at open markets, and hiking to the Tiger's Nest, a sacred sanctuary notched precariously in a sheer cliff wall. Visiting a farmhouse, we sip yak butter tea with a friend of our host. She has rarely seen westerners in her valley. At the moment there are nine monks chanting blessings for her family, their low monotones droning through a smoky curtain in an adjacent room. Invited to join them, we duck into the dark, candle-light chamber. They press closely together on the floor to make room. A few of them glance at us briefly, as if it's common to be joined by a gaggle of people from the other side of the planet. As Buddhists, they pray for all sentient beings. Little do we realize how timely this is.

That evening a troubled American approaches our table in the hotel dining room. He's just called home. It's September 11, 2001 and 9:30 am in New York. Since we have no access to news, we learn nothing more until the next morning when we're leaving on our trek and are followed by a dozen children. I ask them why they're not in school. *Because two big buildings in America fell down, madam.* The King has closed the schools and government offices so people can light butter lamps, in mourning. As we begin our ascent, I carry the news of America and the King's compassion like a ponderous backpack.

When we reach the high altitude passes my supplications are all the more fervent. May the miracles that have protected Bhutan fly on these winds to shelter us all. May we create a world safe for children to wave greetings to aeroplanes. May the illusion of separation be lifted so we can find compassion within ourselves. May we keep places of silence, peace and mystery for the whole world to remember. May those who govern do so wisely.

Hob Osterlund, 55 years old, Clinical nurse, comedian and writer, Hawaii

Favourite Hobbies: Performing, photography, hiking

Favourite Country: Bhutan

Favourite Book: Red by Terry Tempest Williams, My Story as Told by Water by David James Duncan

Other Publishing Experience: Many professional articles

About Eye Books

Eye books is a young, dynamic publishing company that likes to break the rules. Our independence allows us to publish books which challenge the way people see things. It also means that we can offer new authors a platform from which they can shine their light and encourage others to do the same.

To date we have published 30 books that cover a number of genres including Travel, Biography, Adventure and History. Many of our books are experience driven. All of them are inspirational and life-affirming.

Frigid Women, for example, tells the story of the world-record making first all female expedition to the North Pole. A fifty year-old mother of three who had recently recovered from a mastectomy, and her daughter are the authors neither had ever written a book before. Sue Riches is now both author and highly sought after motivational speaker.

We also publish thematic anthologies, such as The Tales from Heaven and Hell series, for those who prefer the short story format. Here everyone has the chance to get their stories published and win prizes such as flights to any destination in the world.

And here's what makes us really different: As well as publishing books, Eye Books has set up a club for like-minded people and is in the process of developing a number of initiatives and services for its community of members. After all, the more you put into life, the more you get out of it.

Please visit www.eye-books.com for further information.

Other Titles by Eye Books

Further Travellers' Tales From Heaven And Hell is the third book in the series. If you would like to find out more about the other two books or any of our other titles please visit our website:

www.eye-books.com

You will also be able to find details on our new titles including:

Riding The Outlaw Trail
Desert Governess
The Last Of The Nomads
First Contact
All Will Be Well
Special Offa
The Good Life
Green Oranges On Lion Mountain
Baghdad Business School
The Con Artist Handbook
The Forensics Handbook

Special Offers and Promotions

We are offering our club members and people who have read this book the opportunity to take advantage of promotions on our other books by buying direct from us.

For information on these special offers please visit the following page of our website:

www.eye-books.com/promotions.htm